Other books by Ted Wachtel

Author

True Representation:
How Citizens's Assemblies and Sortition Will Save Democracy

Dreaming of a New Reality:
How restorative practices reduce crime and violence,
improve relationships and strengthen civil society

Real Justice:
How We Can Revolutionize Our Response To Wrongdoing

The Electronic Congress:
A Blueprint for Participatory Democracy

Co-Author

Toughlove

Toughlove Solutions

The Restorative Practices Handbook
for Teachers, Disciplinarians and Administrators

Restorative Circles in Schools:
Building Community and Enhanced Learning

Restorative Justice Conferencing:
RealJustice© and the Conferencing Handbook

Family Power:
Engaging and Collaborating With Families

Building Campus Community:
Restorative Practices in Residential Life

Editor

Safer Saner Schools: Restorative Practices in Education

Beyond The Schoolhouse

◆◆◆

Learning For A New Reality

by
Ted Wachtel

published by

THE PIPER'S PRESS
Pipersville, Pennsylvania • USA

BEYOND THE SCHOOLHOUSE: LEARNING FOR A NEW REALITY

Copyright © 1977, 2020 The Piper's Press
All Rights Reserved

FIRST EDITION

THE PIPER'S PRESS
P.O. Box 400
Pipersville, PA 18947 USA

Edited by
Mary Shafer

BuildingANewReality.com Book Series
ISBN-13: 978-1-934355-40-4
ISBN-10: 1-934355-40-2

PRINTED IN THE U.S.A.

*For Susan, Josh and Benjamin,
and all the kind people who have helped us along the way.*

Table of Contents

PROLOGUE ix

BEYOND THE SCHOOLHOUSE

1. SKATING AWAY 3
2. COMPULSORY EDUCATION 7
3. A CENTURY OF COERCION 11
4. AIMS AND MEANS 15
5. MEASURING THE MARIGOLDS 19
6. LINES THAT DIVIDE 25
7. THE CLOISTERED CLASSROOM 31
8. TOO MANY BLACKSMITHS 35
9. WRITING ON THE WALL 39
10. FREEDOM OF EDUCATION 43

TOWARD AN INTEGRATED MIND

11. SOMETHING ELSE 49
12. SPLIT BRAIN 53
13. A CHANGE OF MIND 57
14. B-I-T-S A-N-D P-I-E-C-E-S 63
15. ELECTRIC MEDIA 69
16. COSMIC CONSCIOUSNESS 75

17. AGE OF GENIUS 83
18. SEEING THE FOREST 91
19. CHILDREN AS PEOPLE.. 95
20. LIFE AS LEARNING 101

LEARNING BY EXPERIENCE
21. THINGS YOU CANNOT SEE 109
22. REALITY 115
23. THE REVOLUTION 121
24. LEARNING SYSTEMS 125
25. BEING OUR OWN HEROES 131
26. ALL THE KIND PEOPLE 137
27. DREAMING OF A NEW REALITY 139
28. A PRACTICAL MATTER 145
29. FUTURE WITHOUT LIMITS 147
30. A NEW DAY 149

EPILOGUE 151
NOTES 157
ABOUT THE AUTHOR 171

Prologue

As an angry young man in 1975, I quit my doctoral program in Educational Media. The next year, I quit my job as my school district's media coordinator. I had worked for eight years in Pennsylvania public schools as a history teacher and administrator. I had a good experience working with some wonderful people, but I also had a growing realization that there were better ways to serve the best interests of young people than existed in schools.

On July 4, 1976—coincidentally, the 200th anniversary of the Declaration of Independence—I declared my own independence. That day, my wife Susan and I and our two young sons said goodbye to our house—which would soon belong to someone else—and left for Laguna Beach, California, in a camper van.

Although we found worthwhile work opportunities there, the emotional pull of family and friends drew us back to Pennsylvania.

There, in 1977, Susan and I founded the Community Service Foundation, an alternative school for delinquent and at-risk youth.

That same year, I finished writing *Beyond the Schoolhouse*, my first book. It's about what I felt was wrong with our educational system, and why and how I'd like to change it. When I completed the book, I put it away on a shelf and have only shared it with a few people since. I did not publish it because I was not yet confident enough about my ideas—however strongly I expressed them in the book—and because I was afraid I might offend school officials involved in sending young people to our new alternative school.

Four decades later, schools are struggling with the same problems, only more so. But in the meantime, I have validated my proposed solutions in challenging school settings around the U.S. and the world. The time has come to get my book off the shelf and into readers' hands.

In the interest of clarity, I have included some modern comments—akin to editor's notes in a critical edition—in the Notes section. These are intended to provide current context for some important points, demonstrating the material's continued relevance even as the issues evolve.

I am not anti-school. I am against the schools' monopoly on resources for learning, and the ridiculous belief that the best learning only occurs in school settings—a mindset which dismisses the value of self-directed learning and learning by doing.

I applaud the many people who enjoy school learning and thrive in schools, but millions of people do not like school and do not thrive there. Yet children are forced to go to school anyway, like indentured servants who labor under adverse conditions—day after day, year after year—until they finally earn their freedom.

Chris Mercogliano, author of *How to Grow a School*[1], explains: "The regrettable truth is that the majority of children have only one option, tuition-free schools that are part of a monolithic system operating according to a highly rigid educational model that very often runs counter to how children actually learn and grow, and that almost entirely ignores the vast variation that exists among them."

Whether public, private, parochial or charter, most schools rely on the same assembly line, top-down approach to learning that characterized schools implemented in the 19th century. Such a rigid approach to learning does not meet many students' needs, and fails to keep pace with a changing world.

The concerns I expressed in 1977 are still valid. After more than forty years of experience, working with difficult students and struggling teachers and schools, I can say with assurance that learning should not be limited to schools…that we need to think "beyond the schoolhouse."

Ted Wachtel
Pipersville, Pennsylvania
March, 2020

PART **ONE**

Beyond The Schoolhouse

It is the business of an intelligent theory of education to ascertain the causes for conflicts that exist and then, instead of taking one side or the other, to indicate a plan of operations proceeding from a level deeper and more inclusive than is represented by the practices and ideas of the contending parties.

John Dewey, 1938[2]

BEYOND THE SCHOOLHOUSE: Learning In A New Reality

CHAPTER 1

Skating Away

The Arizona highway seemed an endless blur, edged by desert sand and topped with a starry night sky. Sue, Josh and Benjie slept behind me in the van while my thoughts flew back to Pennsylvania.

Angry thoughts. Confused thoughts. Replaying the events which led to my resignation from the public schools and our present journey.

Some of the events were books. Books that jarred my consciousness and pushed my head in new directions. Books like *Deschooling Society* (1971)[3], which advanced the idea that schools should be abolished, that they have dehumanized learning and removed it from the flow of life.

"School appropriates the money, men and good will available for education and in addition discourages other institutions from assuming educational tasks. Work, leisure, politics, city living and even family life depend on schools for the habits and knowledge they presuppose, instead of becoming themselves the means of knowledge."

I read Ivan Illich's book while pursuing my doctorate in educational media and began to doubt my own purposes. Said Illich, "In the United States the per capita costs of schooling have risen almost

BEYOND THE SCHOOLHOUSE: Learning In A New Reality

as fast as the cost of medical treatment. But increased treatment by both doctors and teachers has shown steadily declining results."

George Gallup, the famous pollster disagreed. "Education is still regarded as the royal road to success in life,"[4] he said, in an address to a group of educators in 1975. "The most convincing proof of America's support for the schools, however, is to be found in the public's readiness to levy heavy taxes on themselves to maintain and to improve their schools."

I wish Mr. Gallup had been with me in the spring of 1976, as I faced an audience of angry taxpayers and explained the library and audiovisual budgets for the upcoming school year.

In communities throughout the nation, taxpayers have been voting down bond issues and budgets, holding mass rallies against higher school taxes, and in some cases have shut down their local schools by cutting off funds.

These tax revolts do not demand an end to schools as Ivan Illich suggests, but call for schools as "they used to be." More discipline, less permissiveness, cut out the frills, hold the line on spending, get back to basics. Citizens seem to be reacting to the events of recent decades which brought consolidation, integration, federal funding, new math, open classrooms, student rights and teacher strikes.

Bewildered by changing values, shocking violence, rising costs and declining academic standards, much of middle America wants to return to the educational situation of yesteryear and questions the prevailing assumptions of the school establishment, that more money and new techniques means better education. In fact, many feel quite the opposite, that schools are providing less for more money.

A coyote at the edge of the road brought me back to Arizona and I noticed the sky brightening behind me. Well, I was no longer with the public schools. Having found myself among those who question the effectiveness of schools, I resigned and with my family, sold our home and headed for California. Before we left, I jokingly consulted the *I Ching*, an ancient Chinese fortune-telling book, and was surprised by its specific response. "We see dense clouds but no rain coming from our borders in the West."[5]

With the California border ahead, I popped a Jethro Tull tape in our portable player, slipped on the earphones and settled back into my thoughts about schools.

My fellow educators, whose salary increases of the last decade bear the brunt of the taxpayer's wrath, defend their gains as long overdue and blame parental permissiveness, too much television, lack of respect for authority, inflation, reduced federal funding, court interference and other external factors for the problems the schools are facing.

Through the 1960s, the debate about "what's wrong with schools" centered around reforms within the public schools and attempts to develop alternative and free schools. Public school reform has dwindled with reduced federal funding and the alternative school movement has quieted also. Only private schools have benefited from the public schools' woes, as many disenchanted parents have decided to buy their children's education.

The problem, as I see it, is that we have come to confuse learning with schooling. We think that the only way people can be educated is by attending school. Learning is measured by the number of years spent in schools and the number of diplomas collected. Informal learning, acquired through direct experience, is regarded as inferior to school learning. The modern world, whose money is the measure of all things, rewards those with diplomas more generously than those without, and spends a large part of its income on schools.

We are coming upon a new day. We must reexamine our most cherished institutions, and determine whether they really meet our needs. If they do not, we must have the courage and the will to respond differently. If schools no longer serve us well, then we must look beyond the schools.

BEYOND THE SCHOOLHOUSE: Learning In A New Reality

I heard my family stirring awake as the sun rose in the rearview mirror. We crossed into California, and I pulled out the earphones on the tape player. Jethro Tull's vocals filled the van.

One day you'll wake up in the present day
A million generations removed from expectations
Of being who you really want to be.
Skating away, skating away
Skating away on the thin ice of a new day.

CHAPTER 2

Compulsory Education

The day before I started my first year of teaching, I put the following quotation from George Santayana[6] on the bulletin board, in ominous black letters. "Those who cannot remember the past are condemned to repeat it." The quotation stayed up for several weeks until I changed it to a display of historic political cartoons.

One day a pleasant girl in one of the tech school sections asked me about the quotation.

"I just want to train horses. Why must I study history?"

I proceeded to explain the importance of learning from the past, of analyzing events and actions that have occurred, in order to make better choices when faced with similar situations.

She persisted. "But Mr. Wachtel, what if I don't really care about all that? I don't even know if I want to vote. Why must you make us study it? I'll forget it all anyhow."

I could not answer her question. I still can't. Why not just teach history to those people who want to study history? Why do we force people to study anything against their will? Especially when they probably do what they want to do and not what we try to make them do. Despite all the schools' efforts, many students graduate high school without even learning reading, writing and arithmetic.[7]

The question persisted throughout my experience in the public schools, appearing in varied circumstances, but never so bluntly as when I went through my old test files the year after I switched from history teacher to district audiovisual coordinator.

As I looked over the tests, there were several questions on each test, specific "facts" of history that I could not remember or about which I felt unsure. When was the meat-packing act passed? I could remember the novel, *The Jungle*, that helped bring it about. And when did the Spanish-American War end? Was it the same year, in 1898, or did it carry into the next?

If I couldn't remember or if I felt hesitant, why was it so important that kids learn it? After all, I was the specialist. Perhaps the problem was the kind of test. I tried many things that year in my search for truth: from multiple-choice to essay, graded to pass/fail, lecture and textbook to simulation game and field trip.

Whichever subject content or teaching method or evaluation tool I chose, I still faced the same dilemma. I could not get kids who didn't want to learn something to learn it. And if I forced them with bad grades and other coercive means, would the negative attitude fostered be worth the little information they would regurgitate on a test and then forget?

But I persisted. Perhaps I could find a way to make kids like history. Because my history students were members of the television generation, I used films. When I couldn't get the films I wanted, I made my own slide productions, with contemporary music in the soundtrack. As audiovisual coordinator, I instigated a new social studies course with several colleagues. We obtained federal funding for large quantities of audiovisual materials, individual projectors and cassette-filmstrip players.

Over several years, the course experimented with a variety of techniques, activities and grading systems. Although these efforts seemed to improve interest over traditional methods, most students were still motivated only to the extent that they were required. I had difficulty determining what really worked and what did not.

Not until I stumbled upon James Herndon's book, *How to Survive in Your Native Land* (1971)[8], did I finally realize the fallacy of coercion: "As long as you can threaten people, you can't tell whether or not they really want to do what you are proposing that they do. You can't tell if they are inspired by it, you can't tell if they learn anything from it, you can't tell if they would keep on doing it if you weren't threatening them. You cannot tell."

I know very few teachers who would agree with an end to compulsory education, and I suspect that most see such a proposal as a threat to their jobs. But I also know that every teacher who ever taught would be delighted to enter a classroom filled with interest and motivation, rather than indifference and resistance. The only way that will ever happen is by changing the laws that require children to attend school. Until then, we will find the schools trying to deal with many students who resent being led to water and cannot be made to drink.

BEYOND THE SCHOOLHOUSE: Learning In A New Reality

CHAPTER 3

A Century of Coercion

The Greeks first established schools as a general preparation for citizenship, unlike earlier schools in Egypt and Babylonia which were vocational, preparing individuals for priesthood or civil service. Whether the Greek schools were successful, I do not know, but the idea persisted through Western history. On the walls of the Thomas Jefferson Memorial in Washington is inscribed, "Establish the law for educating the common people. This it is the business of the state to effect and on a general plan."[9]

Education has been a fundamental ideal of the United States since its beginnings, but it was not until 1852 that Massachusetts made public education mandatory[10] and free. Other states passed laws requiring children to attend school and not coincidentally, soon established taxes to support the decision.

If compulsory schooling was a good way to educate citizens, one could not tell that from the lives of the founding fathers. Jefferson himself had received his earliest education confronting nature on a frontier plantation. His academic studies were largely tutorial, even at college with Dr. William Small, the mathematician, and in law with George Wyeth, the learned judge.[11] George Washington and Benjamin Franklin were running plantations and starting printing business in their teens.

Although public schools of the 1850's became compulsory, at least they were small. By the time I hit the public schools, a century later, they were big. Industrialization, urbanization, automation and suburbanization had turned America into an assembly line and schools reflected the trend. I never attended a school of less than 500 students and my high schoolmates numbered almost 1000.

Even in rural America, the "consolidation" movement[12] closed the one-room schoolhouses and small high schools, in an effort to achieve "efficiency" and "better facilities." The secretary who worked with me in the media center had seen her small high school close in time for her graduation in 1954. She laughed about how their gowns were whitened by the cement dust on the floor of the high school's not-quite-finished auditorium.

When I first met her, she was serving as a secretary in her former high school, a small building which was used as an instructional materials center for the consolidated school district. I could see the hurt in her eyes when visiting school administrators laughed at the fact that the former chemistry lab in the basement had only a six-foot ceiling and the business education department had been housed in a renovated chicken coop. There was nothing lacking in her life that a new high school would have provided and I cannot imagine a larger school preparing her more adequately for her job, as I have never known a more diligent and self-reliant worker.

Bigger is not better, as far as I can see. An older teacher, who taught at the other high school replaced in 1954, once expressed to me his concern with the high school of 1500 students we now occupied. It was a hot spring afternoon and we were trying to keep the lid on a group of two hundred students in a study hall. He remarked that on such a day, classes in the old high school would have been abandoned and everyone would have gone outside to play baseball — students and teachers. "I knew every student personally and informality was possible."

A few weeks after writing the preceding paragraphs, I read an Associated Press story (April 14, 1977) headlined on the front page of the local *Morning Call* with "That little red schoolhouse is looking better and better. A National Institute of Education study reported, "But even with all their spending and all their new resources, rural people still did not generally receive that which they wanted most dearly — better life chances for their children. Those chances are more affected by the "education and income of parents, the social and economic character of the community, the investment of time energy and love by many adults, and plain luck than they ever are (or were) by the size, newness or variety of the local school."[13]

What the public schools achieved in the first one hundred years of compulsory education was the dehumanization of learning. The conditions which I encountered in the 1950's, as a member of the postwar baby boom, were so far removed from the original aims of Thomas Jefferson that he would not have recognized them as the means for accomplishing his ideas. Instead he would have recommended an end to compulsory education with some other words that are inscribed on the walls of his memorial. "We might as well require a man to wear still the coat which fitted him when a boy, as civilized society to remain ever under the regimen of their barbarous ancestors."

BEYOND THE SCHOOLHOUSE: Learning In A New Reality

CHAPTER 4

Aims and Means

If the aim of the public schools in a democracy is to prepare individuals for citizenship, then American schools have lost their way. They have confused the original Greek ideal with the accumulation of knowledge. Ask a principal for an evaluation of his school and he is likely to cite the latest standardized test results.

"Sometimes one sees in the schools simply the instrument for transferring a certain maximum quantity of knowledge to the growing generation. But that is not right. Knowledge is dead; the school, however, serves the living...the aim must be the training of independently acting and thinking individuals."[14]

The author of these words, Albert Einstein, had one of the greatest minds of this century, but he failed mathematics in a German high school. His problem was not serious, for he taught himself calculus and analytical geometry in his early teens. Thomas Edison, generally recognized as the world's greatest inventor, entered the public schools in Port Huron, Michigan. The teacher considered him a dunce, and he left school after three months, never to return.

Schools do not encourage independent acting and thinking. According to Robert M. Pirsig, "they teach, you imitate." I remember a teacher's disapproving eyes when she saw the title of the book I was reading. *Zen and the Art of Motorcycle Maintenance* (1974), said *The New York Times*[15], is "profoundly important...full of insights into our most perplexing contemporary dilemmas." A bestseller. Oh, then it must be all right.

Pirsig continues: "If you don't imitate what the teacher wants, you get a bad grade. Here, in college, it was more sophisticated, of course; you were supposed to imitate the teacher in such a way as to convince the teacher you were not imitating, but taking the essence of the instruction and going ahead with it on your own. That got you A's. Originality, on the other hand, could get you anything from—A to F. The whole grading system cautioned against it."

In the grading system schools have developed the "carrot and stick" principle of motivation to perfection. Not only do we force young people to be somewhere we want them to be, but we also pit them against one another in a competitive struggle for the teachers' approval. But it is much easier to foster academic diligence by fostering rivalry than by fostering curiosity. And if the grading system does not keep the student on the right track, teachers have a wide range of punishments they may impose, from detention and humiliation to brutal beating.

In my twenty-five years in schools, I have seen students made to stand in corners, halls, closets and wastebaskets. I have seen teachers strike students with wooden sticks, often indiscriminately, as if handing out chocolate kisses. I wore a black and blue mark for several weeks, punished for forgetting my gym shorts in my locker. The teacher meting out the punishment would stand by the entrance to the locker room and dispense stinging swats, occasionally just for "kicks." If he did that on a street corner, he would be arrested. But in the school, he was protected.

I have seen students refused passes to go to the toilet, with no apparent justification, and an entire student body limited to the use of one set of toilets because some students had been smoking in the other. I have seen punishment carried out without the slightest opportunity for the student to defend his innocence and for infractions of the rules that were, at best, picayune.

Court decisions in recent years had brought some semblance of civil rights to the schools, but in May, 1977, Richard Nixon's appointees tipped the Supreme Court scales back toward cruel and unusual punishment. According to Justice Powell, writing for the 5-4 majority, "corporal punishment serves important educational interests."[16] The constitution does not protect public school students from beatings by teachers, even though it protects criminals from the same punishment.

Justice White challenged "the extreme view of the majority that corporal punishment in public schools, no matter how barbaric, inhumane or severe, is never limited by the Eighth Amendment… If it is constitutionally impermissible to cut off someone's ear for the commission of a murder, it must be unconstitutional to cut off a child's ear for being late to class."

Despite Justice White's objections, the prevailing law of the land now prescribes beating as an educational technique, a decision called "incredible" by a spokesman of the National Parent-Teacher Association. The American Federation of Teachers, however, greeted the decision "with pleasure."[17]

Perhaps the public schools use violence because they are frustrated with their impossible task: compulsory education. Students forced to be students cannot be relied on for their own motivation. They must be coerced.

But one cannot expect to prepare people for democratic citizenship by practicing tyranny. The simple truth is that people learn what you do, not what you say. In terms of democracy, forcing people to learn is as foolish as forcing them to vote.

BEYOND THE SCHOOLHOUSE: Learning In A New Reality

CHAPTER 5

Measuring the Marigolds

I entered the first grade in 1952, on the hundredth anniversary of compulsory free schooling in America, the same year I saw the motion picture *Hans Christian Anderson*,[18] starring Danny Kaye. I think the movie made a greater impression on me, because I remember it vividly, while I have few recollections of first grade.

Early in the film, there is a musical scene in which the great Danish storyteller sings a song about an inchworm, while school children sing their arithmetic tables. I would like to share the words with you, because I know of no better way to describe my perception of the public school's attitude toward children:

> Inchworm, inchworm
> Measuring the marigolds.
> You and your arithmetic
> You'll probably go far.

BEYOND THE SCHOOLHOUSE: Learning In A New Reality

Inchworm, inchworm
Measuring the marigolds.
Seems to me you'd stop and see
How beautiful they are.

"If you cannot count it, it does not count," is the official school motto. Without measurement, schools would not be schools. I estimate that I spent between one and two full school years in formal test situations between kindergarten and the end of my graduate school education, not to mention informal evaluation. I can think of no other situation in life in which I have been under such scrutiny. If you feel I exaggerate, then let's ask the question: "How do schools measure thee?" Let me count the ways.

One. Kindergarten testing. One has to give schools credit: They get right to the point. The very first experience a child had with the school district in which I worked was a visit to the elementary school, to be tested for "kindergarten readiness." On the basis of this evaluation, usually carried out by one of the elementary school administrators, the school recommended whether a child should begin learning or not.

Two. Skill progress tests. These were the tests I took every year in elementary school, through which I learned to be proficient in the skill of IBM test marking. I was fortunate enough to be born in to the age of high speed scoring devices and computers, so that learning to mark multiple choice and true-false boxes with a number two pencil was a fundamental step in my education.

Three. Intelligence tests. One of the biggies; recorded in a special spot in your permanent file. From these scores, the school can tell how smart you are. The fact that it has little to do with real life, that it measures how fast you can do certain mental tasks in a sterile environment, does not make the emphasis on I.Q. scores inappropriate—for those are precisely the conditions that prevail in school.

Four. Objective tests. These count for grades and include several varieties: multiple choice, true-false, matching and fill-in-the-blank. Many teachers prefer them because they are quick to grade. The students who prefer them can memorize, guess or cheat well.

Five. Essay tests. These also count for grades. Some teachers prefer them because they feel essays reveal the depth of a student's understanding. The students who prefer them can bullshit well.

Six. Open book tests. I never could understand these. Regardless of the subject matter, they seem to measure how well someone can look something up in hurry. Having learned about indexes in library class helped a lot.

Seven. Homework and labwork. My personal unfavorite because I rarely turned it in on time. Systems for counting homework and labwork as a grade vary widely among teachers, but one fact is universal: Kids won't do it, if it doesn't count.

Eight. Term papers. My personal favorite, because I usually turned them in on time. They are closely related to essay tests, in that they are preferred by bullshitters. They are required in high school English and History, because they will be required in college English and History. Why they are required in college is beyond me, for I have never written one since. They are probably helpful in preparing for a writing career in one of the enterprising firms that sell term papers to college students.

Nine. Creative effort. This is very difficult to assign a grade, but art teachers do it all the time. My creative effort included highly original excuses for not doing my homework.

Ten. Class participation. Also very difficult to assign a grade. Typically, the emphasis is placed on how often you say something, rather than what you say.

Eleven. Final examinations. Usually objective tests, because they can be scored quickly. The report card deadline leaves teachers with less time to grade final examinations than any other test given during the year, despite the fact that final examinations count much more heavily than any other tests.

Twelve. Personality tests. These are the kind of evaluations that are supposed to identify your personality traits from paper and pencil activities, verbal responses, and your reaction to inkblots.

Thirteen. Guidance tests. The Kuder Preference Test[19] was my favorite. It asked questions like: "Which would you rather do? Fiddle around with test tubes, operate on human brains, clean fish, or sign checks?" Then you pushed a pin through a dot on the green sheet to make your choice. The guidance counselor would use the Kuder Preference Test Kits to predict your future from the pattern of your pinholes.

I remember how the guidance counselor shook her head when she handed back my Kuder Preference Test. "Atypical," she said. Which meant that my response patterns weren't covered by the Kuder Preference Test Kit. That was too bad, for if she had the right data, I am sure that she could have told me that I was perfectly suited to be a dropout educator.

Fourteen. College boards. The Super Biggie. The measurement that makes the difference between Harvard and Meadowlark Junior College. In the days when the postwar baby boom was overwhelming higher education, the college boards could make the difference between college or not. Now, many colleges will take whomever pays tuition.

Fifteen. Quizzes. Usually employed by teachers as a threat to make sure that you did your reading assignment. They come in two varieties: the announced quiz and the infamous pop quiz, which comes without warning (unless you are in a section that holds class after lunch, in which case you not only have warning, but also the answers).

Most tests are written by teachers who pay no attention to scientific evaluation procedures or are so subjective as to make the grade a matter of whim. Usually no one dares challenge the teacher's subjective judgment, although I remember a fellow in college who telephoned the poet to verify his own interpretation of a poem against the teacher's. The teacher was wrong and had to change the test grade, but such audacity is uncommon.

The variables affecting grades are so uneven from place to place and teacher to teacher, that a comparison between an A at Harvard and an A at Meadowlark Junior College is absurd. Yet grades continue to be the focus of school activities. They must be, for without them schools would lose their most important coercive tool.

If you are not convinced of the foolishness of all this measurement, imagine the techniques of the schools applied to a child learning to talk. Instead of letting the natural process unfold as the child hears others speak and sorts out the words and grammar through direct experience, the child would be tested for talking readiness, annually assessed for talking progress, divided into listening groups according to I.Q., evaluated with a quarterly grade and assigned verb forms to practice in the playpen. Based on the schools' success with reading, we could reasonably expect a dramatic increase in the numbers of stutterers and mutes.

Constant evaluation creates anxiety and inhibits interest. Children hate learning when they are always scrutinized and corrected. A garden of growing flowers does not need to be counted, weighed and measured: it just needs a healthy environment. With all their measurement, teachers, guidance counselors, psychologists and administrators only block the sunshine and step on a lot of marigolds.

BEYOND THE SCHOOLHOUSE: Learning In A New Reality

CHAPTER 6

Lines That Divide

Jefferson Elementary School, which I attended in the late fifties, had a pair of separate entrances marked "Boys" and "Girls." Though no longer used as separate entrances, they symbolized a fading reality. Before World War II employed millions of women in industry, a distinct line segregated males and females into separate roles in society. The exploits of "Rosie the Riveter" altered a stereotype of the American Woman that had been challenged by woman suffrage, and has been shattered by women's liberation. Despite persistent discrimination, a new reality is clearly in the making.

Similarly, the line segregating races has been confronted. The 1954 Supreme Court decision that separation is inherently unequal, still echoes through the nation's schools. Although implementation of that ruling has not been easy, educational policies that draw lines between people of different races are no longer acceptable.

But schools still draw lines. They distinguish between people by age, ability and academic status, in ways that are inherently undemocratic and that interfere with the natural processes of learning.

The most obvious lines are based on age. Somehow, schools have arrived at the conclusion that people learn in accordance with

BEYOND THE SCHOOLHOUSE: Learning In A New Reality

the number of times they have orbited the sun since their birth. After the fifth time around, children enter kindergarten; after the sixth, they enter first grade; and so on.

A "curriculum" dictates what children will learn each year. Certain knowledge and certain skills, according to schools, are appropriate only at certain ages. One year might include addition and subtraction, while another covers multiplication and division. One year the child meets the Pilgrims, another year the Greeks. The fact that in real life, children crawl, walk, talk, control their bowels, count, and ride bicycles at different ages does not deter schools from forcing children to learn the same thing, in the same way, at the same age.

There is no such thing as "third grade history" and "fourth grade math." These are abstractions based on arbitrary lines, drawn by human beings and not by gods. Perhaps an assembly line society feels more comfortable believing that learning can be packaged in uniform boxes, of uniform quality, uniformly aged. But in truth, children suffer unnecessarily the clumsy attempts of schools to fit them between the lines.

I have listened to grown men and women debate at length the merits of a middle school with grades 5 through 8, versus the merits of a middle school with grades 6 through 8, versus the merits of a junior high school with grades 7 through 9. I still cannot understand why they think that it would make any difference. Where in nature are these lines they draw?

There is no other situation in life where people are physically arranged in chronological age groups, with each year's activity carefully prescribed. The school's idea of "learning in unison" is contrived and unnatural, and so is the anxiety caused in children and parents who are led to believe that there is something wrong if a child cannot keep the pace.

The lines based on age are crisscrossed by lines based on ability. Within each grade, students are divided into top, middle and bottom classes; or within each class, students are divided into top, middle and bottom groups. Schools call this process "homogenous grouping," an educational practice supported not by research, but by convenience. Homogenizing students makes it easier to teach the same thing, in the same way, at the same age.

Stigma is the price paid by students for teachers' convenience. When human beings are treated like categories, they tend to act like categories. Educational research has found that when groups are deliberately mislabeled, without the knowledge of teachers or students, students seem to perform according to their labels.

Teachers are aware of the stigmatizing effects of grouping. Many have been taught to avoid obvious classifications like "top, middle and bottom." Instead they name their reading groups "bluebirds, robins and sparrows." It takes kids about one day to figure out which are top, middle and bottom.

Even more obvious are special groups. I was in a special group for six years. The "opportunity classes" were selected by I.Q. tests and grades for an accelerated academic program. I don't know which was worse: when we acted like arrogant brats harassing an inadequate teacher, or when we were ridiculed as "eggheads" by other students. I do know it was worse to be ridiculed as "dummies," the nickname for the un-accelerated group. The school, of course, didn't call the group "dummies." They called the group "special education," which also takes kids about one day to figure out.

Recently, a high school student related a personal example of another special group experience. He remembered that as an elementary student, he had desperately avoided using his faulty "R" in his interview with the speech therapist, but was finally forced to reveal it. He felt more embarrassed by the conspicuous weekly therapy than by his speech defect. He may have been justified by more than his feelings. A school speech therapist once confided to me that many of his students would probably resolve their own speech defects[20] by growing older.

One of the reasons expressed most often for sending kids to elementary school is for "socialization." I looked up the word in the Random House Dictionary and found that it is the noun form of the verb "socialize," which means "to make social; make fit for life in companionship with others." I could not understand how grouping together thirty children of the same age and test-taking ability provides "fitness for life in companionship with others."

I decided to look up the word "social." The first definition said "pertaining to, devoted to, or characterized by friendly companionship or relations." That certainly does not apply to schools, for they are characterized by competition for group membership and grades. And how can students socialize, when most of the day they are not permitted to talk to each other?

But reading further, I found the appropriate meaning. The fifth definition is "pertaining to human society, especially as a body divided into classes according to worldly status: social rank." Human stratification is the socialization that goes on in schools. Democratic socialization cannot occur where arbitrary lines segregate children from one another.

Besides social stratification, high school life is fragmented by other lines that divide the day into forty minutes of History, forty minutes of English, forty minutes of Study Hall, forty minutes of Math, thirty minutes of Lunch, forty minutes of Gym.

If you can keep your lunch down, gym class offers twenty minutes of vigorous exercise and twenty minutes of vigorous clothes-changing and showering. Arriving wet and sweaty to Industrial Arts or Home Economics, there is just enough time to get everything ready for work, when the bell rings for forty minutes of Whatever, followed by forty minutes of Whichever.

The unnatural fragmentation of the high school schedule may be a good preparation for ulcers, but not for a healthy life. It may duplicate the pace and pattern of many jobs, but one chooses those jobs and gets paid for enduring them. Students do not get paid for enduring school. They do not choose to endure the lines that schools draw between them and through them. Nor do they choose to endure the most pervasive line of all: the compulsory line that divides learning from life and young people from the world beyond the schoolhouse.

BEYOND THE SCHOOLHOUSE: Learning In A New Reality

CHAPTER 7

The Cloistered Classroom

In 1975, the year before I quit working in the public schools, an article appeared in an official Pennsylvania Department of Education publication, which shocked me with its candor: "But as living patterns changed and specialization took over, learning became catalogued exclusively under 'schools.' Now students spend years cloistered in the classroom, then have to go out into the world and function as adults, regardless of the fact that many times they don't quite know how to go about it."

Behind this frank assessment from the agency charged with supervising Pennsylvania's schools was the Secretary of Education, John C. Pittenger[21], whose ideas conflicted with most educators' acceptance of the sterile isolation of classroom learning. "We want to bring about student participation in the learning process—more learning by doing. And for this to happen schools will have to be more flexible in allowing for a greater use of out-of-classroom experiences."

BEYOND THE SCHOOLHOUSE: Learning In A New Reality

He would have received a warmer welcome in law enforcement circles. In a background paper for Department of Justice grants, juvenile justice officials said: "Youths are frequently prevented from assuming meaningful and productive roles in society...The child's only social requirements commonly are staying in school and staying out of the way of the real world. While he is in school, a child is not responsible for any task, any service or any socially valued product."

If a youth achieves good grades or membership in a status group at school, such as the football team or school choir, the youth's school experience may be tolerable or enjoyable—but for those who do not "succeed" at school, they are trapped in a hostile environment which labels them as failures.

A recent remark by Willie Mays illustrates the prevailing attitude toward young people in schools. Attributing the Mets' winning streak of early June, 1977 to the relaxed leadership of the new manager, Joe Torre, he explained, "He treats his players like men, not schoolboys." For in the artificial world of the schoolhouse, it is acceptable to treat human beings differently than in the world beyond.

I began my higher education at a state university in Ohio in 1964 when college women had curfew at ten o'clock on weeknights, eleven on Friday night, and midnight on Saturday. Men could live in apartments but even private accommodations were subject to inspection by the infamous "Seekies," the campus security police who patrolled for signs of women visitors and other infractions of the rules. Although many college students were twenty-one years of age, everyone was subject to the school's paternalistic policies until they graduated. A cloistered college student, I found that high school friends who chose jobs and apartments over college education had adult roles long before I completed my extended adolescence.

The shock waves of campus unrest changed the nature of campus life in the late Sixties, but an incident at the high school where I taught in 1969 sheds light on the lunatic fringe of high school cloistering. Issues of *Time* and *Newsweek* carried covers depicting feature articles about the sexual revolution in America. The now-retired Superintendent of Schools ordered the covers removed from the copies in the high school library, to protect children from obscenity they were likely to find in their own homes.

In my years as a student in the public schools, I was protected from democracy and freedom of speech. Schools then and now create phony governments for students to make believe that they are making decisions. The Student Council can do anything it wants except what the administration doesn't want—such as criticism of the school.

A young man I know published an independent magazine for high school students which was characterized by integrity, excellent artwork, and a diversity of viewpoints. Nonetheless, he was harassed by his high school principal until he asked the local American Civil Liberties Union to send a letter to the school explaining the constitutional right to freedom of the press.

Schools don't like learning experiences they cannot control. When I initiated a student community cable television station that pipes video programs from the high school into local residences, the most common question I heard from teachers and administrators regarded the method of censorship I was going to employ, never considering the possibility that we could trust high school students to demonstrate common sense and self-restraint.

The public schools also protect students from "unpleasant" facts of history, such as the Pilgrims' slaughter of the Native American population, or "disloyal" skepticism about government, such as the Vietnam and Watergate eras warranted. With one exception, my high school teachers left me totally unprepared to deal with fallen Presidents, the humbled CIA and FBI, and clayfooted congressmen.

Conspicuous are the skills I never learned in public school: income tax preparation, gardening, minor auto repairs. I learned sines and cosines, memorized the innards of a foetal pig, and imitated the teacher's critique of T.S. Eliot—none of which is useful to me now.

Marshall McLuhan, in *The Medium is the Message* (1967),[22] pointed out the high level of information outside the school, versus the low level within. "Today's television child is attuned to up-to-the-minute 'adult' news—inflation, rioting, war, taxes, crime, bathing beauties—and is bewildered when he enters the nineteenth century establishment where information is scarce but ordered and structured by fragmented, classified patterns, subjects, and schedules."

Students would love to escape the classroom. Philadelphia's experimental school-without-walls, called the Parkway Program,[23] once had 15,000 applicants for its 500 enrollment. But Pennsylvania's effort to promote out-of-classroom learning has departed to Harvard with John C. Pittenger, leaving things much the way he found them.

Perhaps the most insidious evil of the cloistered classroom is its tendency to force upon students an unfair exchange. In a recent debate with a defender of school learning, the individual lamented only the fact that schools had not required him to learn to play the piano. This person, as so many products of school learning, traded his confidence in his ability to learn by himself for the school's paternalistic guidance, a most uneven value.

CHAPTER 8

Too Many Blacksmiths

Since the Iron Age, the blacksmith has been plying his trade. Until the Industrial Revolution, he made tools, hardware and a diversity of iron objects on his anvil—but factories eventually assumed most of his work. By 1900, the blacksmith was largely a farrier, putting iron shoes on horse hoofs.

The blacksmith, however, did not learn his trade at school. He learned by doing, usually as a helper or apprentice. He did not have formal lectures, took no paper-and-pencil tests and received no grades. No diploma certified his right to be a blacksmith, and the quality of his work had nothing to do with the name of his alma mater.

As the Industrial Revolution advanced, learning on the job was replaced by schools, as the blacksmith was displaced by factories. Systems, rather than individuals, became the popular reality. The path to almost every occupation became a classroom setting. People now believe that years of theoretical knowledge should precede practical experience and that the students in schools should hold information in their heads until the distant day that they are allowed to use it. The grades achieved in acquiring that theoretical knowledge are the major criteria for predicting success in an occupation.

Psychologist Calvin W. Taylor has been investigating the relationship between school grades and career performance. In a study[24] that compared doctor's grades during college and medical school with a set of 77 on-the-job performance measures devised in collaboration with a medical school dean, there was no significant relationship between grades and performance. On several measures, in fact, the relationship was negative; that is, the higher an individual's grades in college, the poorer his performance on the specified task. "This is a somewhat shocking finding for a medical educator like myself," said the dean.

A few months ago, I listened to a young medical student rant and rave about the inadequacy of his medical school preparation, about highly paid medical professors who were more interested in research than teaching, about mimeographed lectures and irrelevant instruction. After reading Calvin Taylor's findings, I am convinced that the young man was justified in his angry assessment.

In another study with scientists at the National Aeronautics and Space Administration, Taylor confirmed what previous studies had already shown.[25] "The relationship of undergraduate college grade-point average to success as a scientist has been shown by many investigations to be, at best, low."

In my own informal survey, I found that most people feel they did not learn the important aspects of their profession until they began to practice it. In teaching, I can see little connection between what I learned in school and what I eventually had to do on the job. Education professors were among the worst teachers I ever had, and with few exceptions, put themselves in the hypocritical position of telling their students to do as they said, not as they did.

One of the fundamental flaws of career training is that it postpones direct experience until one is almost finished with the educational program, although one is expected to select an occupation years in advance. In junior high, I spent a great deal of time worrying about what I was going to be when I had no first-hand experience with the careers I was considering.

The result of this circumstance is that people invest their lives in expensive and time-consuming career preparation without knowing if they are suited for that occupation. I have witnessed the trauma of student teachers who had their first practical experience after almost four years, only to find that they "unraveled" in the classroom. Their tragic desperation felt like a dead friend.

I know scores of people who found that they hated the career they thought they would pursue. One individual became a carpenter after one year of teaching and another prepared to be a printer, but ended up driving a diaper service truck. The cost in wasted resources to both the individual and society is awesome.

Some might argue that the schooling is not wasted, that the person has had a "broadening" experience. But there are lots of broadening experiences in life. Imagine the world travel one could accomplish for the cost of a college degree.

Perhaps we might better accustom people to learning jobs by direct experience, rather than preparing them for a single occupation. For even if people like their career, there is no guarantee of an opening after they graduate. There is also the likelihood that a chosen occupation will someday be rendered obsolete.

Technical schools on the high school level are expensive imitations of the real world that arbitrarily decide which industries they will serve. Some industries have their personnel trained for them while others must train people themselves. The taxpayer should not have to bear the burden of business. But technical schools are popular among young people because they come closer to direct, purposeful experiences than any other kind of school.

The teaching profession offers an excellent illustration of the failure of school to respond to the needs of the real world. In the

BEYOND THE SCHOOLHOUSE: Learning In A New Reality

1960s, a shortage of teachers prompted schools to expand teacher training programs and encourage teaching as a career. The result, as the shortage became a surplus, was a glut of teachers on the job market. Not only is it almost impossible for a young teacher to get a job now, but a veteran teacher who wants to change jobs has almost no chance of finding another position.

Ironically, many teachers and other college graduates thought they could improve themselves by acquiring more degrees, only to find that their masters and doctorates priced them out of the job market. The United States now has a multitude of college degree holders sitting around like overripe fruit.

Physicians, however, found that by limiting enrollment in medical schools, they could squeeze the supply of doctors until the demand became overwhelming. Now doctors command incomes that are almost beyond belief.

Diplomas are more like fraternity pins than certificates of competence. As one colleague described the situation in urging me to complete my doctorate in education: "You either want to be a member of the club or you don't."

Diplomas also serve as an easy cut-off point for personnel managers, although the diploma may have nothing to do with the position. I remember my mother telling me that during the Depression, Macy's department store in New York only hired saleswomen with college degrees. You can tell how much progress the schools have made since then, for in the next Depression, Macy's can hire only Ph.D.s.

Schools are like Soviet Central Planning. They do not respond easily to silly notions like demand and supply. Their adjustments are clumsy and years late. If schools dominated occupational preparation in the early 1900s the way they do today, the Model A Ford would have replaced the Model T before schools realized that the automobile was here, the horses gone, and that they were graduating too many blacksmiths.

CHAPTER 9

Writing on the Wall

The schools I entered in the 1950s are not very different from schools today. They still put you in a classroom and believe that you will learn important things there. They still tell you that they are preparing you to be a good citizen, despite their failure to practice good citizenship. They still tell you that they are preparing you for a meaningful career, despite the failure of millions of graduates to obtain jobs in any way related to their training.

But the myths of schools are wearing thin. No matter how much money we pour into them—and we have squandered billions—they do not fulfill their golden promises. Even though the students of my generation have spared the schools the continued pressure of growth by having few children, shrinking enrollments seem to be viewed as a threat rather than an opportunity. For private colleges, the threat is very real since their competitors—the public universities—have a monopoly on taxpayers' money, and private colleges are dropping like flies.

The state universities are in trouble also. College education is not compulsory and young people have turned away from higher education in increasing numbers. Many prefer to travel or work at different jobs or pursue independent reading as an alternative means of learning. I suspect that some of the same alternatives would be pursued if high school education was not required.

Self-preservation has become the most important issue, and in the public schools where compulsory education prevails, the threat has assumed the form of violence. According to the Associated Press (February 26, 1977) "an estimated $600 million is spent each year as a result of vandalism in schools. This is more money than was spent for textbooks in 1972 and is enough to hire 50,000 more teachers."

Senator Birch Bayh, chairman of the subcommittee on juvenile delinquency which released a comprehensive study of school violence,[26] said that, "While certainly not every school in the country is faced with serious crime problems, it is clear that for a growing number of students and teachers the primary task is no longer education, but preservation."

"Even more shocking is the 70,000 serious physical assaults on teachers and the literally hundreds of thousands of assaults on students perpetuated in our schools annually."

Several days after reading the article, I heard Maxwell Davison, a juvenile court judge, astutely observe at a hearing on changing Pennsylvania's juvenile statutes, "We need to take a hard look at whether our schools are doing enough in a way of providing alternative schooling for those juveniles who are obligated to comply with compulsory school attendance laws and indeed re-examine the compulsory attendance laws themselves."

According to Gary Kocher (*Morning Call*, Allentown, PA, January 11, 1977), Pennsylvania will not be questioning the idea of compulsory education. "Curbing school violence will require alternative programs and more money. A Pennsylvania Department of Education task force studying violence and vandalism in schools has submitted its recommendations."

The recommendations included creating an advisory committee, identifying schools with severe problems for special attention, funding programs based on the number of disruptive students in a district, pooling of effort among schools with a small number of disruptive students, identifying potentially disruptive students during elementary school, using alternative methods such as in-school suspensions, resource rooms, special counseling, alternative schools and education day treatment facilities, and the training and employment of security personnel, parent aides, student incentive programs and building alterations. All cost money.

Not one word was mentioned about questioning compulsory education. Perhaps it is inappropriate to ask schools to question their own existence. It is very much like asking Richard Nixon to conduct an investigation of his own administration's wrongdoing.

But the problem of schools will not go away. They are likely to intensify and those watching the turmoil are likely to be increasingly unsympathetic. For it will become apparent that administrators and teachers alike are more concerned with their own vested interests than with examining the roots of their students' discontent.

"School reform," which tempted the nation to spend federal money on education, has proved untenable. Little change resulted from the effort and more money is unlikely to improve the situation. What is required is a fundamental reassessment of why we have schools, how learning really occurs, and what we can do to make our educational practices more consistent with reality.

While schools fiddle, young people are burning. The violence is so widespread that *School Product News* has begun to resemble a magazine for crime control rather than education. Alarm devices, unbreakable windows, and security card systems are advertised on the same pages as floor sweepers and playground equipment. The most incredible product advertised was a special gadget that a teacher wears around the neck at all times and which sends a signal to the main office for reinforcements if the teacher is attacked.

We cannot continue to forced young people to attend school. The experience of my own generation with schools does not lend much support for compulsory education. Although the postwar crop has mellowed since its youthful protests against the Vietnam War, we have not forgotten the injustices and inadequacies of schools.

With the median age of Americans pushing thirty, the baby boom is growing up and will change this nation, not by protest marches, but through the quiet business of living. For some indication of the new majority's sentiments, schools might listen to the words of "Kodachrome," a popular tune released by song-poet Paul Simon on his album (*There Goes Rhymin' Simon*, 1973) which has become a bestseller.

> *When I think back on all the crap I learned in high school,*
> *It's a wonder I can think at all.*
> *And if my lack of education hasn't hurt me none,*
> *I can read the writing on the wall.*

CHAPTER 10

Freedom of Education

About three hundred years ago, an English Quaker founded a colony in what was to become the United States. In doing so, he introduced a radical concept in an age when people were required to practice the religion of their monarch: He allowed people to choose for themselves.

William Penn's colony[27] became one of the few populated places on the face of the earth where human beings could follow their own beliefs rather than the dictates of government. Philadelphia, its largest city, was a center for the development of freedom and witnessed the adoption of the Declaration of Independence and the Constitution.

Ignorance is a traditional enemy of freedom, so it was not surprising when Pennsylvania became a leader in education. The well-meaning citizens of the state were among the first to implement schooling for all children. But freedom is a tricky business, and sometimes the institutions that we plant and nurture to enhance freedom contain the seeds of new oppression.

BEYOND THE SCHOOLHOUSE: Learning In A New Reality

In the middle of the nineteenth century, when schools became popular, the information level in American society was low. The Industrial Revolution was just cranking up and media technology was still primitive. Newspapers were unreliable and books were scarce. Besides, many people were illiterate. At the time, schools were among the best places to be exposed to information and at least, to learn to read.

If schools had confined themselves to basic skills, perhaps they would not be as oppressive as they are. In the past century, they have tried to monopolize learning. But they cannot compete any longer with the explosion of information brought about by high-speed printing, satellites, computers, film, radio and especially television.

Schools served the needs of the Industrial Revolution. They conditioned Americans to the demands of the factory and assembly line, and "Americanized" the children of successive waves of immigrants. Public school was the great unifier. Every child spent some time in school, pledged allegiance to the flag, spoke English, heard about the Pilgrims and George Washington, and hopefully learned a few basic skills. Today television is the great unifier; Cookie Monster and Big Bird are the All-American Teachers.

Times have changed, but the schools have not. They symbolize conformity and the American trend toward bigger-than-human institutions. Their efforts at "democratic training" are typified in my own mind by a recollection of my kindergarten experience with reciting the pledge of allegiance. Every day, for the first year of school, I pledged my allegiance to the flag and "to the Republic for Richard Stands." Sometime in the first grade I got around to asking who Richard Stands was.

By the time I started teaching in the Pennsylvania schools, they had fully assumed the old role of the church as the official oppressor. They control access to almost every occupation and consume a large chunk of the national income. They dominate people's lives from pre-school to adulthood and brainwash them with a sterile view of life and learning. Even private schools are regulated to be like public schools. James Herndon[28] (*How to Survive in Your Native Land*, 1971) wrote, "The public school is the closest thing we have in America to a national established church, Getting-An-Education the closest thing to God."

I don't believe in schools. I don't approve of the way they deal with children, and I don't want my children to attend them unless they choose to attend. I'm not un-American, just unorthodox. But if I don't send my children to school the government will send me to jail, like the English government sent William Penn to jail for being a Quaker.

Perhaps we should follow Herndon's suggestion for dealing with the public school. "It should be possible to treat it and deal with it as the church has been treated and dealt with…There's no law any more that people must go to church or pay attention to the church, and so many people don't while others do. That is the best you can expect, and good enough."

I suspect that if public schools were no longer compulsory, most kids would still go to them. Although I don't approve of schools I certainly defend the right of people to attend them. I also defend the right to suicide. As William Douglas[29] once wrote: "The true sponsors of the Free Society are those who defend the advocates of creeds they despise."

I like to think of myself as a true sponsor of freedom. I do not believe that true freedom is anything you can get away with, like running naked down Main Street and not getting arrested. Rather, I feel that freedom must be tempered with regard for other people. Like running naked through a nudist colony, a nudist beach or through your backyard in the dark, carefully avoiding the birdbath.

Compulsory schooling does not only limit American freedom. Every nation in the world that can afford schools forces them on children. Even in places where they don't have freedom, they have schools.

BEYOND THE SCHOOLHOUSE: Learning In A New Reality

Perhaps history has come full circle, for there are few populated places on the face of the earth where human beings can follow their own educational beliefs rather than the dictates of government. In an age when people are required to follow the educational practices of the state, we need "freedom of education," a radical concept like that which William Penn introduced in his colony three hundred years ago: Allow people to choose for themselves.

PART **TWO**

Toward An Integrated Mind

So what do you think is education?
Is it to help you fit into the mechanism
Of the present order, or disorder of things?
Or do you think it should be something else?

— *Krishnamurti, 1970*[30]

BEYOND THE SCHOOLHOUSE: Learning In A New Reality

CHAPTER **11**

Something Else

The day John F. Kennedy died, Lee Harvey Oswald blew a hole in my American Dream. Oh, sure, I knew about tragedy: the Civil Rights struggle in the South, people waking up dead on the streets of Calcutta. But we were going to take care of all that, me and Jack. As soon as I finished school, I was going to join the Peace Corps and help primitive people in jungle villages and be a savior. Or, if the times required, I would join the Army and fight for freedom and be a hero. After that, I was going to be a politician and pass laws that would make everything better, and be a President.

I believed in the American Dream. I believed in Congress and the FBI and the CIA and the U.S. Marines. I believed in General Electric and its slogan: "Progress is our most important product." I believed in superhighways and skyscrapers, in air conditioners and automobiles. And though I knew our government had made mistakes in the past, like breaking treaties with the Indians, that was all behind us. We were a mature nation now, and acted only out of the highest of motives. After all, we were the biggest and the best, and nobody killed presidents in America anymore.

BEYOND THE SCHOOLHOUSE: Learning In A New Reality

Several months after the assassination and several weeks before graduation, I crossed paths with an old friend, Rick. He had been a tentmate at overnight camp, but I hardly saw him in our high school of three thousand students. He acquired a sudden notoriety as we approached diploma time; telling off teachers, talking about going to Greenwich Village with his guitar and harmonica instead of finishing high school. People were amazed, because Rick had always been a sensitive, quiet fellow and a conscientious student.

I don't know what drew us together at that time, but I found myself at Rick's home one night, persuading him to finish high school. I suppose he listened to me because I listened to him. I suppose he saw some merit in my argument because I saw some merit in his.

He did finish high school and a bit of college—but he went off and did what he wanted anyway, and as best I could tell when I last heard of him, he was enjoying himself. But I know that our discussion was not pointless, for Rick got me thinking about the possibility that although "school" and "career" were the prevailing American Dream—there might be something else.

Nonetheless, I believed in school. I never liked it much, but I could be pretty good at it when I wanted to be. Besides, school would get me where I was going.

So I packed my bags and went to college in Ohio. While I was there, President Johnson told the nation that, after unprovoked attacks on Americans by North Vietnam, he was sending in the troops. We now know that he was lying, but at the time, it all seemed pretty reasonable. I never considered the possibility that a president would tell Americans something that wasn't true.

I was home when I heard about David, another friend. I knew him through his sister, with whom I shared nine years of public school. David had tried a college in New England, but didn't like it much, so he enlisted in the Army. President Johnson sent him to Vietnam and he came back a hero. A dead hero.

Something Else | **chapter 11**

I sat with other people in the church and listened to the minister read excerpts from David's letters. Shortly before he died in the A Shau Valley, David wrote something very strange: that he felt like a Nazi invader burning defenseless villages on the Russian steppes.

For a long time, I wondered whether David had died for nothing. One day, I realized that he hadn't. He had touched other people, including me, with his words and left us questioning things that we had always accepted blindly. Most of us live out our entire natural lives and never accomplish that.

I was in graduate school, doing my intern teaching at a Pennsylvania high school, when my oldest, closest friend told me he wasn't bothering to finish college. Randy said that he only had two term papers between him and his diploma, but he felt that his degree was irrelevant to his life. I didn't understand what he meant.

He lived in Seattle, where he had gone to college, so I only heard from him occasionally. He was managing a small, co-op grocery store, and had settled down with a woman he met doing anti-war work. I should have understood this decision, for it was not unlike my decision to teach rather than manufacture furniture with my father.

Some years later, in 1975, I visited Randy with my family. Susan, Josh, Benji and I were tenting across the country, looking up old friends and making new ones. Our experiences confirmed my doubts about my old American Dream. And the co-op was a prosperous food market, which by the money measures of the modern world, made Randy's alternative dream a big success.

But I was tired of the modern world. Years of trying to "reform" the public schools had worn me to a frazzle. So had all the fruitless campaigns for fruitless politicians and fruitless issues. So had Chicago and King and Bobby. Jackson State and Kent State. Then Watergate. And six years of doctoral studies in Educational Media, now hanging in the air.

I had finished all the work for my dissertation except the final writing. Although I enjoy writing, I could not bring myself to complete and sign a research study that, in my heart, I knew was bullshit. So we bought a tent and went West for the summer.

Like so many others before us, we were looking for America. And we found it.

Swimming in the green Wisconsin river, sweating through the Badlands lunarscape, sunsetting on the Oregon coast…the journey reawakened our sense of awe and appreciation for the natural reality that underlies the disorder of modern life.

Reading from *Black Elk Speaks* (1932),[31] a Sioux elder's account of the invasion of his homeland, while we followed the Little Bighorn to the rolling hills of Custer's doom. Photographing buffalo from a Jeep, remnants of herds that had once carpeted the Plains. Seeing the faces on Mount Rushmore with armed park rangers, circling helicopters, and realizing that when we carved our presidents into the Plains Indians' sacred mountains, it was as if someone had chiseled Marx, Lenin, Stalin and Khruschev into the bluffs at Niagara Falls. Visiting the Pine Ridge reservation, home of the Oglala Sioux, a week after the shootout with the FBI and feeling unwelcome. The matter of "breaking treaties with the Indians" is not all behind us.

As I stood with my family at the Wounded Knee Cemetery, I sensed a common source in my growing feelings and the militancy of young Sioux: a sense of shared longing for a dream that preceded the chugging juggernaut of industrial civilization. And I thought of Black Elk's description of the 1890 massacre at Wounded Knee Creek:

"I can still see the butchered women and children lying heaped and scattered all along the crooked gulch, as plain as when I saw them with eyes still young. And I can see that something else died there in the bloody mud, and was buried in the blizzard. A people's dream died there. It was a beautiful dream."

CHAPTER **12**

Split Brain

While I was learning the Pledge of Allegiance, the edge of science was splitting the mammal brain. About twenty-five years ago at the University of Chicago, Roger Sperry and Ronald Myers cut the connection between the two halves of a cat's cerebrum[32] and found that each hemisphere functioned as an independent brain. Although subsequent findings with humans proved even more dramatic, schools remain largely ignorant of this radical change in our understanding of learning and intelligence.

In the initial experiments, the cat's optic chiasm was cut to separate its left and right eyes, while its left and right "brains" were divided by severing the corpus callosum, the bridge between hemispheres. With one eye covered, the cat learned a simple task. When the cover was switched to the other eye, the cat did not recognize the task. The second half of the brain had to learn the task as if it were a second cat.

Vietnam was coming to a boil in the early Sixties, when Sperry and Michael Gazzaniga studied humans whose brains had been split[33] to control epilepsy. In a series of cleverly designed experiments, they discovered differences between the left and right

53

hemispheres, including confirmation of speech and language comprehension centers in the left half, as identified by Pierre Paul Broca and Carl Warnicke[34] in the nineteenth century.

In one experiment, a female split-brain patient laughed at a picture of a nude woman shown to her left hemisphere and said that she saw a nude woman. When the picture was revealed to the right hemisphere, the woman said that she saw nothing, but smiled and chuckled. Apparently capable of emotional response, the right side could not name what it saw.

In a related experiment, the patient could pick a spoon from a group of objects after seeing a picture of a spoon with the right brain, but could not say the word. Even with a spoon in her hand, the patient could neither name nor describe the picture nor object.

In his *Scientific American* article (August, 1967)[35], which appeared a few months before I graduated from college, Gazzaniga summarized the split-brain experiments:

"All the evidence indicates that separation of the hemispheres creates two independent spheres of consciousness within a single cranium, that is to say, within a single organism. This conclusion is disturbing to some people who view consciousness as an indivisible property of the human brain."

His conclusion was not disturbing to anyone I met the next year in the public school; at least, no one ever mentioned it.

As science defines the differences between the hemispheres, the dominance of the left hemisphere in modern civilization becomes obvious. The left is logical and analytical, concerned with mathematics and words. The right is artistic and holistic, concerned with spatial relations and music.

The left hemisphere is associated with social order and politics, the right with the mystical and supernatural. Although left-brain functions seem to be most valued in our society, the right brain seems to be involved with such important capabilities as creativity and intuition.

An article[36] on "The Other Hemisphere" by Robert Trotter (*Science News*, April 3, 1976) affirmed the dominance of the left hemisphere in urban culture, but cited Solomon Katz's study[37] of the Inuit Eskimos, who seem to favor the right. Parallel attributes of our two brains were listed:

LEFT HEMISPHERE *(Right side of body)*	**RIGHT HEMISPHERE** *(Left side of body)*
Speech/Verbal	Spatial/Musical
Logical, Mathematical	Holistic
Linear, Detailed	Artistic, Symbolic
Sequential	Simultaneous
Controlled	Emotional
Intellectual	Intuitive, Creative
Dominant	Minor (Quiet)
Worldly	Spiritual
Active	Receptive
Analytic	Synthetic, Gestalt
Reading, Writing, Naming	Facial Recognition
Sequential Ordering	Simultaneous Comprehension
Perception of Significant Order	Perception of Abstract Patterns
Complex Motor Sequences	Recognition of Complex Figures

Because the left side of the brain controls the right side of the body, the vast majority of right-handed people might illustrate the dominance of the left hemisphere.

According to the article, "some types of drug use may be related to attempts to temporarily free the right hemisphere from the left's dominance."

An incidence of marijuana use reported in Carl Sagan's new book, *The Dragons of Eden* (1977)[38], offers a strange insight into the phenomenon of two brains.

The individual felt the presence of a silent "watcher" and he asked it silently, "Who are you?"
It replied, "Who wants to know?"
Humanity wants to know.
Understanding the human mind is our most fundamental quest. The investigation to date has revealed a deprived hemisphere. In an article[39] on the state of brain research, Roger Sperry wrote in *Engineering and Science* (January, 1974):
"Our educational system and modern society generally (with its heavy emphasis on communication and on early training in the three R's) discriminates against one whole half of the brain...In our present school system, the attention given to the minor hemisphere of the brain is minimal compared with the training lavished on the left or major hemisphere."

Yet more than two decades after Sperry's original experiment, his discoveries do not impress the schools. In the spring of 1976, during my last weeks in public education, I informally polled more than a dozen school administrators from several districts to determine how many were aware of the concept of "two brains." Not a single administrator was aware of hemispheric research or its implications for improving human learning.[40]

CHAPTER **13**

A Change of Mind

I have always pictured the origins of human consciousness before the construction of the pyramids and ziggurats of ancient civilization. The advent of agriculture produced the food to sustain urban population, and the advent of language provided the words to establish social order. Because the capability for speech in most human beings is located in the left half of the brain, I assumed that the logical, linear, detailed, sequential and analytical functions of the left hemisphere have dominated our existence since the dawn of civilization.

But I have had a change of mind. After scrutinizing the archaeological and physiological evidence, a Princeton psychologist has determined that human consciousness arose several thousand years after the first civilizations. Early intelligent people did not think as we do, but were told what to do in novel situations by an area of the right hemisphere that corresponds to the area for speech in the left hemisphere.

They experienced auditory hallucinations, the "voices of the gods," which have faded in most human minds with the rise of written language, but which persist in the minds of schizophrenics and can still be induced by religious frenzy, drugs, or electrical stimulation of the right hemisphere.

Julian Jaynes' book[41], *The Origin of Consciousness in the Breakdown of the Bicameral Mind* (1976), was favorably reviewed in *Time* shortly after I began writing this book, and was in its fifth printing by the time I obtained a copy. An endorsement on the jacket was written by the author of my college psychology text, the eminent Ernest R. Hilgard[42], and critics were talking, like Christopher Lehmann-Haupt[43] of *The New York Times*: "Who is Julian Jaynes anyway…and why is he saying such brilliant things in his first book instead of in the crowning volume of a long and illustrious career?"

Teaching at Princeton, Jaynes has pursued a lifelong fascination with the notion of consciousness. His carefully reasoned and researched book has toppled the theories of many other psychologists.

Drawing from the same split-brain experiments, archaeological findings, and ancient religious literature that are available to any interested thinker, Jaynes demonstrates that the first intelligent human mind was "bicameral," not dominated by the left hemisphere, as we are today. The evolution of conscious speech in the left hemisphere was balanced by the development of unconscious speech in the right hemisphere.

The day-to-day life of bicameral people was much like driving a car for many modern people, passing without conscious thought but involving decisions, stopping and starting, reacting and reasoning. In a novel or stress situation, such as at a crossroads on an unfamiliar route, the right hemisphere of the bicameral mind would voice its conclusion. The contemporary mind, however, consciously ponders the situation, experiences the anxiety of feeling lost, and finally makes a deliberate decision. I have often found that the best decision is made unconsciously, turning in the direction of vague feeling rather than conscious thought.

A Change of Mind | chapter 13

The right hemisphere in the bicameral mind transmitted its conclusion to the left hemisphere through the anterior commissure, a small bridge between halves of the brain, using the information code of the times: spoken words. The voice of the right hemisphere sounded within the bicameral mind and moved the individual to action.

An old Sumerian proverb suggests the process: "Act promptly, make your god happy." Translated by Julian Jaynes, it is saying: "Don't think; let there be no time space between hearing your bicameral voice and doing what it tells you."

Jaynes supports his theory with ample archaeological evidence. He traces the rise of agriculture and language from the Incas to the Egyptians, citing the common practice of burying leaders as if they were still living, with food, furniture, and often servants. Kings were related to gods, for their words echoed in the bicameral mind long after death.

The Egyptians put their dead king in a pyramid with his worldly possessions, where he reigned as Osiris, the name for a dead king. In life he had ruled as Horus, as would his son. The hallucinated voice of Osiris merged with the voice of Horus, repeated for generation after generation.

Jaynes explains how, unified by a common language and common culture, the individuals in bicameral civilization had no sense of self. Working like a colony of ants and guided by the recurring voices, bicameral civilizations were capable of colossal construction projects spanning many generations of effort. They obviously mastered engineering techniques and mathematical calculations requiring sophisticated reason, but did so without conscious thought.

The breakdown of the bicameral mind occurred after the development of written language, and was sometimes hastened by floods or volcanic eruptions, which forced bicameral people into migration and association with other cultures. If one meets people who are distinctly different from oneself, one becomes aware of one's self.

But writing was the source of dominance by the left hemisphere in newly conscious humanity. The intangible spoken word was overwhelmed by the specific, tangible properties of the written word. Language could now be stored, hidden, rendered permanent, private or precise. The voices of the gods began to fade.

"About 1230 B.C., Tukulti-Ninurta I, tyrant of Assyria, had a stone altar made that is dramatically different from anything that preceded it in the history of the world... No king before in history is ever shown kneeling. No scene before in history ever indicates an absent god. The bicameral mind had broken down."

Jaynes offers this event as stark proof of a change of mind. The absence of gods undermined the king's authority and the modern notion of rebellion became possible. Tukulti was burned to death in his newly built city, by rebels under the leadership of his own son.

The authority of the gods was replaced by the authority of fear and military might, a dilemma which persists today. "Militarism, police, rule by fear, are all the desperate measures used to control a subjective conscious populace, restless with identity crises and divided off into their multitudinous privacies of hopes and hates."[44]

Jaynes states that, "In the bicameral era, the bicameral mind was the social control, not fear or repression or even law. There were no private ambitions, no private grudges, no private frustrations, no private anything, since bicameral men had no internal 'space' in which to be private...All initiative was in the voices of the gods."

Almost frantically pursuing the gods, people invented prayer, astrology, divination and omens. The right brain is still associated with the religious, mystical, and supernatural concerns of humans. But Jaynes provides his strongest proof in terms of the written word itself, especially in the religious writings of an ancient people who weathered the breakdown of the bicameral mind and recorded their religious feelings at different intervals in a book which we use today: The Bible.

Although many books of The Bible are considered compilations of more than one writer, most scholars regard Amos, dating from the eighth century B.C., and Ecclesiastes, from the second century B.C., as authentic. Compare the two:

> *AMOS*
> *And they shall plant vineyards, and drink the wine thereof; They shall also make gardens, and eat the fruit of them. And I will plant them upon their land. And they shall no more be plucked up out of their land which I have given them. Saith the Lord thy God.*

> *ECCLESIASTES*
> *And I hated all my labour wherein I labored under the sun, seeing that I must leave it unto the man that shall be after me. And who knoweth whether he will be a wise man or a fool? Yet will he have rule over all my labours wherein I have shown myself wise under the sun. This also is vanity.*

Like the Greek heroes of *The Iliad*, Amos was directed by God. Ecclesiastes directed himself, like the Greek hero Ulysses in the epic Odyssey, who defied the supernatural to make his way home from the wars. Although Greek literature confirms the existence and breakdown of the bicameral mind, The Bible provides the most complete evidence.

Julian Jaynes demonstrates that intelligent humans have experienced a change of mind within the last two thousand years or so. Driven further into the left brain by the rapid development of vocabulary, logic, printing and technology, the human species may be functioning with a deprived right hemisphere.

BEYOND THE SCHOOLHOUSE: Learning In A New Reality

For those who feel that we lack a proper balance, that we are too dominated by self-consciousness, Jayne's conclusions suggest the possibility that if we changed once, we can change again, returning to a more harmonious consciousness; an integrated mind.

That possibility rests with a resurgence of the right hemisphere, a need expressed in an ancient Psalm: "My mind thirsts for gods! For living gods! When shall I come face to face with gods?"

CHAPTER 14

B-i-t-s a-n-d P-i-e-c-e-s

T-h-e a-l-p-h-a-b-e-t b-r-o-u-g-h-t a-b-o-u-t t-h-e f-r-a-g-m-e-n-t-a-t-i-o-n o-f h-u-m-a-n l-i-f-e. M-a-r-s-h-a-l M-c-l-u-h-a-n w-r-o-t-e t-h-a-t "O-u-r h-a-b-i-t o-f t-h-i-n-k-i-n-g i-n b-i-t-s a-n-d p-a-r-t-s—s-p-e-c-i-a-l-i-s-m—r-e-f-l-e-c-t-e-d t-h-e s-t-e-p-b-y-s-t-e-p, l-i-n-e-a-r d-e-p-a-r-t-m-e-n-t-a-l-i-z-a-t-i-n-g p-r-o-c-e-s-s i-n-h-e-r-e-n-t i-n t-h-e t-e-c-h-n-o-l-o-g-y o-f t-h-e a-l-p-h-a-b-e-t."

As we moved from voice to print, we changed the way we perceived the world and the way we lived in it. We divided the world into nations, land into property, people into categories, work into jobs, and life into education, career, and retirement. After years of school, we graduate into our specialized task, work for a few decades, then retire into uselessness.

I once asked an Eastman Kodak machinist what kind of projectors he made. He didn't know. He just made bits and pieces, never knowing the meaning of his life's labor.

Jobs and schools are the inventions of the alphabet age, beginning with literate civilizations in Babylonia, Egypt, and Greece. Since the printing press put words on an assembly line, school has come to resemble an assembly line. Dividing learning into groups and grades, subjects and curricula, with specialized teachers and uniform units of instruction, schools shuffle "normal" learners along the line at a uniform rate until they are graduated into jobs.

Because written words were largely the product of the left half of the human brain and there was no reciprocal development in the right half, our culture has been dominated by the left brain for many centuries. Defined by split-brain experiments in the last quarter-century, the characteristics of the left brain clearly bias the schools. Madeleine Hunter[45] wrote in *Today's Education* (November/December 1976) that findings "powerfully suggest that schools have been beaming most of their instruction through a left-brained input (reading and listening) and output (talking and writing) system, thereby handicapping all learners."

And it is no coincidence that art, music, industrial arts and physical education, predominantly non-word, right-brain activities, are known throughout the public schools as "minor" subjects.[46]

One day 2,400 years ago, at the time when schools were just getting started in Greece, Socrates sat on the banks of the Illisis with young Phaedrus, enjoying the cool shade of a tall plane tree and debating the merits of oral truth versus written truth.[47]

The old philosopher told Phaedrus about two Egyptian gods, Theuth and Thamus, who were discussing Theuth's latest invention: the alphabet. Thamus warned him that his discovery would create forgetfulness in the learners' souls; that they would trust to the external written characters and not remember of themselves.

"You give your disciples not truth, but only the semblance of truth; they will be hearers of many things but will have learned nothing."

Phaedrus accused Socrates of inventing this tale of Egypt, but the old man responded that the ancients were satisfied to hear the truth from a rock or tree, "whereas you seem to consider not whether a thing is true or is not true, but who the speaker is and from what country the tale comes."

And that is precisely what schools do. They do not ask the student whether a thing is true or is not true, but who the speaker is and from what country. They are not interested in the learner's sense of truth, but in the manipulation and memorization of words.

Schools cannot change. They cannot serve the right hemisphere in a balanced way, because their very existence and structure is a function of the left hemisphere dominance.

It is the left brain that defines learning as a separate compartment of life, and it is the left brain's obsession with sequence and order that dictates a fixed ladder curriculum and segments knowledge into courses, like canned goods on a shelf. If schools were to shift strongly toward the right brain's attributes, they would cease to be schools.

Where is the right brain hiding? Robert Ornstein,[48] at the Institute for the Study of Human Consciousness, suggests that the left brain dominates our mind like the sun dominates the daytime sky. We can only see the stars of our right brain when the sun sets, but the stars are always there.

However useful the sunshine, too much causes sunburn. Reason and logic are important, but they can blind feeling and dazzle intuition. When adult Americans watched the Vietnam War on television, believing in the logic of saving the Vietnamese people by destroying them, casually eating supper while human beings were blown to bits and pieces on the evening news, they were not feeling their right hemisphere…but many of their children were.

In *The Psychology of Consciousness* (1973),[49] Ornstein cites a Sufi story that illustrates the contrast between logical left and holistic right-brain functions. Written by Idries Shah[50], a contemporary Sufi, this sample from *The Exploits of the Incomparable Mulla Nasrudin* (1972) demonstrates the "school mentality:"

Nasrudin sometimes took people for trips in his boat. One day a pedagogue hired him to ferry him across a very wide river. As soon as they were afloat, the scholar asked whether it was going to be rough.
"Don't ask me nothing about it," said Nasrudin.
"Have you ever studied grammar?"
"No," said the Mulla.
"In that case, half your life has been wasted."
The Mulla said nothing.
Soon, a terrible storm blew up. The Mulla's crazy cockleshell was filling with water. He leaned over his companion. "Have you ever learned to swim?"
"No," said the pedant.
"In that case, schoolmaster, all your life is lost, for we are sinking."

It is no coincidence that swimming is an unconscious muscle activity controlled by the right brain, and grammar is a left-brain function.

The left brain and its servant, the school, have created an imbalance in human intelligence...the kind of imbalance that spawns bureaucracies with assistants-to-the-assistants, and presidents whose truth abruptly becomes "inoperative" or who lie to the citizenry in order that democracy be preserved. The kind of imbalance that breaks work into fragments without meaning and offers fringe benefits like vacation, sick leave, severance pay, medical coverage—all of which benefit workers only when they are not at work.

Our left-brain dominance has built a monstrous war machine in the name of peace, led by more officers in peacetime than in war, and with a pension system that is breaking the bank. Isolated from our feelings and free from each other, we suffer the alienation of little people amidst big things. Isolated from nature, we foul our food, water and air with our own wastes and poisons devised by too much invention and too little intuition. Lacking the holistic sense of the right brain, we see trees, not forest; we see profit, not social consequence.

School began as an attempt to pave a road to a higher human condition, but has turned into a blind alley. If the origins of our dilemma are rooted in the alphabet, then the solution may be a new means of communication. The invention of electric media, from telegraph to television, has altered the dimensions and nature of human intelligence. The fragmented bits and pieces of printed words have been superseded by a flowing electronic stream of voice, music and images. Perhaps we are already following a new path that leads us away from the school's blind alley.[51]

BEYOND THE SCHOOLHOUSE: Learning In A New Reality

CHAPTER **15**

Electric Media

On January 8, 1815, American forces under the command of Andrew Jackson killed or wounded two thousand British soldiers marching on New Orleans. But the tragic slaughter had no military significance; a peace treaty had been signed two weeks earlier[52] in Belgium. With communication limited to the speed of a ship, the contending armies did not get the message until it was too late.

On October 24, 1861, the last two-pound package of mail crossed the rugged terrain between St. Joseph, Missouri and Sacramento, California in the pouch of a Pony Express[53] rider. The legendary mail service collapsed in financial ruin, victim of the telegraph wire, which carried messages across the continent in a split second.

In the decades between the two events, Michael Faraday[54], an apprenticed bookbinder with little schooling, invented the first workable electric generator, and Samuel Morse[55], an art professor, conceived of the electric telegraph while eating dinner at sea. Human communication took a bold step and transcended distance.

Alexander Graham Bell[56] and Thomas Alva Edison[57] both turned thirty in 1877. Bell, a teacher of the deaf, was leasing

BEYOND THE SCHOOLHOUSE: Learning In A New Reality

telephones to his first customers and Edison, an unschooled wizard, had just invented a practical phonograph. Sound could be transmitted, recorded, stored and retrieved as if it were the printed word. The alphabet now had competition.

At the turn of the century, early motion picture producers, including Edison, were thrilling their first audiences while Guglielmo Marconi[58] was beaming radio messages across the Atlantic. Commercial radio stations were established in 1920, but within a decade, motion visuals and over-the-air broadcasting had merged. On July 30, 1930, the Radio Corporation of America began operating an experimental television station in New York City.

As if to make a dramatic break with the past, the Great Depression and World War II suppressed the birth rate in the United States, while postponing successful commercial television. In 1946, the year I was born, both population and television burst onto the American scene. The huge postwar generation was darkened by the shadow of the atomic bomb, and brightened by the light of a new communication medium. Through no choice of our own, we became the objects of history's most rapid transformation of human intelligence.

Television profoundly altered the relationship between the left and right halves of the brain in a generation of American children. Unlike the left-brain civilization into which we and television were born, our right brains tend to be more involved in our consciousness than our parents; and we are potentially more integrative, capable of shifting between the two halves of our brain at will—or, perhaps, using both halves simultaneously.

Printed words, particularly poetry, can evoke the use of the right hemisphere. But television is more central to our consciousness, evoking the use of both hemispheres. Words, film, music, drawings, photographs, voice, poetry, singing: all can be communicated through the medium of television. Television is inclusive, absorbing other media.

"The book is an extension of the eye...clothing, an extension of the skin...electric circuitry, an extension of the central nervous system." Marshall McCluhan's analogy is well-founded, for current electricity was first observed in 1786 by Luigi Galvani when it caused twitching in a dead frog's legs.

Children born after the mid-fifties are likely to be more video-conscious than oldsters like me, who can remember when there wasn't television. My children have watched television since they could focus their eyes. Ellen Torgerson,[59] in *TV Guide* (April 23, 1977), reports that, "By the time a child is 18, he (or she) has spent 11,000 hours in school—and 15,000 hours watching television. The average 18-year-old has used up the equivalent of more than two full years of his life mummified in front of the TV set."

Mummified? Do I detect the harsh words of a left-brain prejudice? Why is a child more mummified watching television than passively reading a book? And why is a child "using up" life with television? Doesn't the printed word consume time?

Television bombards our senses with sights and sounds. The world leaps into our homes and heads, changing our perception of the globe and other living things. We are aware of interrelationships we did not recognize before video expanded our horizons.

My first recollection of television occurred in 1949. At about the time my mother went to the Bronx Hospital for the birth of my sister, I was watching televisions in a neighbor's apartment down the hall. In 1952, we bought our own television when I attended first grade in suburban New Jersey. My father hooked it up to a metal laundry stand until we had an antenna, and I watched through a blizzard of electronic snow. Who cared? We had television!

By 1956, the vast majority of American livng rooms glowed with grey light and a station in Chicago began broadcasting in color. I was in the fourth grade in Pennsylvania and remember watching Dwight Eisenhower's second-term inauguration when an incredible demonstration occurred. To the amazement of a

BEYOND THE SCHOOLHOUSE: Learning In A New Reality

nationwide audience, an exact duplicate of the inauguration was broadcast through the magic of videotape.

Although live television was soon eclipsed by taped programming, the spontaneous power of the medium was still evident when Jack Ruby shot Lee Harvey Oswald, to the amazement of another nationwide audience. The first televised murder and the first presidential funeral starkly confirmed the nature of electronic media. Just as radio created simultaneous experience for a vast audience, television now feeds images to our collective consciousness. We are bound together by electronic media, in sadness and joy.

Television is a global phenomenon. Satellites bounce video signals to all parts of our planet. A half-billion human beings watched Neil Armstrong walk on the moon, and one billion saw the last Olympics. We have shared experiences to talk about, whether we meet someone from Istanbul or Brooklyn.

Where reception is inhibited by mountains and valleys, community cable systems carry the electronic image to homes beyond the fringe, and make possible local program origination on a neighborhood basis. New cable technology can carry a hundred channels on a single wire.

Television cameras and videotape recorders are as common as printing presses, and are used by many schools and businesses. We find ourselves confronted with personal access to videotape and videodisc. The imminent widespread distribution of a television equivalent to the book, only a half-century after the first broadcast, should give us reason to pause. If the written word had developed as rapidly as electronic media, Hammurabi would not have put his famous code on stone tablets four thousand years ago, but would have printed copies for the entire ancient world on a high-speed, multi-color press.

We are changing faster than we have ever changed before. "We cannot tell what is out there beyond the year 2000, but we can sense the power and the direction of the forces that are now playing upon us," says historian William Irwin Thompson. "At the edge of history the future is blowing wildly in our faces, sometimes brightening the air and sometimes blinding us." (*At the Edge of History*, 1971)

Everyone who fought the British at New Orleans is dead now. A small town has become a sprawling metropolis, and atomic weapons dwarf Andy Jackson's artillery like a dinosaur beside a fly. In less time than it takes to stroll down Bourbon Street, a nuclear missile can arc the globe and turn the "Paris of America" into a crater.

We cannot afford to get the message too late.

BEYOND THE SCHOOLHOUSE: Learning In A New Reality

CHAPTER 16

Cosmic Consciousness

While Marconi was transmitting radio signals from England to Newfoundland, Richard Maurice Bucke[60] was publishing *Cosmic Consciousness* (1901). Farmboy, adventurer, gold miner and eventually physician, Bucke served as an asylum superintendent, professor, and president of the American Medico-Psychological Association. In his book, he stated that "our descendants will sooner or later reach, as a race, the condition of cosmic consciousness, just as, long ago, our ancestors passed from simple to self consciousness."

Bucke felt that language had moved humanity from simple to self consciousness, and that something was moving us toward cosmic consciousness, a third form.

"With this form, of course, both simple and self consciousness persist (as simple consciousness persists when self consciousness is acquired), but added to them is the new faculty...a consciousness of the cosmos, this is, of the life and order of the universe."

BEYOND THE SCHOOLHOUSE: Learning In A New Reality

Christ, Paul, Buddha, Mohammed, Dante, Walt Whitman, many others less famous, and Bucke himself had experienced "illumination," and he predicted that increasing numbers of people would have such experience.

"The person who passes through this experience will learn in the few minutes, or even moments, of its continuance, more than in months or years of study, and he will learn much that no study ever taught or can teach. Especially does he obtain such a conception of THE WHOLE...as makes the old attempts to mentally grasp the universe and its meaning petty and even ridiculous."

Four years later, Albert Einstein published his Special Theory of Relativity,[61] which set forth a totally new universe of time, space, mass, motion, and gravitation; and has been characterized as "one of the greatest intellectual achievements in history."

In *The New York Times Magazine* (November 9, 1930), he wrote that: "There is a third stage of religious experience which belongs to all of them, even though it is rarely found in a pure form: I shall call it cosmic religious feeling. It is very difficult to elucidate this feeling to anyone who is entirely without it, especially as there is no anthropomorphic conception of God corresponding to it."

When touched by such a cosmic feeling, the physicist said, "The individual feels the futility of human desires and aims, and the sublimity and marvelous order which reveal themselves both in nature and in the world of thought. Individual existence impresses him as a sort of prison, and he wants to experience the universe as a single, significant whole."

At the time Einstein was writing this article, a scholar and poet, John Neihardt[62], was listening to an aged Oglala Sioux warrior on the Pine Ridge Reservation in South Dakota. Unable to speak English, the old man related the story of his life through his son, and described an extraordinary hallucination that he had as a young boy, troubled by the onslaught of the white invaders.

At the climax of his Great Vision, which was later performed by the tribe as a dance ceremony, Black Elk[63] said, "Then I was standing on the highest mountain of them all, and round about beneath me was the whole hoop of the world. And while I stood there, I saw more than I can tell and I understood more than I saw: for I was seeing in a sacred manner the shapes of all things in the spirit, and the shape of all shapes as they must live together like one being."

Although his vision revealed the plight of his tribe to him, he showed no bitterness. "And I saw that the sacred hoop of my people was one of many hoops that made one circle, wide as daylight and starlight, and in the center grew one mighty flowering tree, to shelter all the children of one mother and one father. And I saw that is was holy."

Black Elk Speaks appeared in 1932 and faded into obscurity until it became a youth classic in the early sixties. In 1971, the book was launched into international bestsellerdom by a television interview with the aging Neihardt on the Dick Cavett Show.

A few months before the interview, Charles Reich[64] published *The Greening of America* (1970)[65], which became a runaway bestseller in both hardback and paperback editions. Reich described the youth rebellion against the corporate state as "Consciousness III." Like Bucke, Einstein and Black Elk, he perceived a new way of looking a the universe.

Consciousness III "promises a higher reason, a more human community, and a new and liberated individual. Its ultimate creation will be a new and enduring wholeness and beauty—a renewed relationship of man to himself, to other men, to society, to nature, and to the land."

I put my copy of Reich's book into a cardboard box and stored it with the rest of our belongings that we did not sell. Susan and I packed the van with sleeping bags, cameras and projectors, cooking gear and clothes, took Josh and Benji, and left our home and my job at the school district behind us forever.

BEYOND THE SCHOOLHOUSE: Learning In A New Reality

We zig-zagged across the country from Ohio to Tennessee, to Arkansas and Texas, through the great deserts to the Pacific. Traveling south of our previous summer's journey, we sensed the consciousness that had been stifled during the last year of our old life...the consciousness crushed by school.

We were not sure of anything, except that I was through with doctoral degree programs and school jobs. I had never heard of Richard Maurice Bucke and had never read anything by Albert Einstein, but I knew, as many of my generation had come to know, that I had to find a niche in our fragmented economic reality that could give me a sense of wholeness. I wanted a role, not a job.

In the sunny months we spent in Laguna Beach, California, we explored many possibilities, but spent much of our time working with some former East Coasters in establishing a learning program for juvenile offenders and pursuing audio-visual projects.

When we weren't working, we were reading on the front deck of our rented beach cottage, enjoying the beach, watching the boob tube, or taking side trips to the San Diego Zoo and Space Museum, Disneyland, or the nearby mountains. Josh and Benji attended a morning daycare program that included arts and crafts, conversational French, and especially playground.

But somehow, we always felt like visitors in the West, never immigrants. Through mountains and plains, rainforest and deserts, we were strangers in a strange land, taking in its beauty and mystery, but feeling a need to return. We had talked about returning for several days, and had even begun making arrangements, when I had an experience that transcended my previous inklings of a new consciousness.

After a night of little sleep, I deliberately stayed awake for a second night with several people, in an attempt to photograph a child's seizure. With my still camera motor drive, I hoped to film a sequence for a slide production about a neurological disorder. I found myself on a balcony overlooking Laguna Beach in the predawn darkness, snapping photographs of the gathering glow.

As my brain gapped, the way tired brains do, dawn climbed the hills and spilled across the beach into the Pacific. The new light struck my sleepless mind, and I saw image that seemed to focus somewhere inside my forehead, rather than before my eyes. Visions of smiling people I knew back East, green fields and mountains, wood and stone, sun and stream flowed through me. Community...the notion left me with a sense of wholeness I have rarely felt...community; not a place, but a feeling; not an entity, but an understanding.

The idea filled a gap in me that longed for closure, providing me with a sense of possibility, like a wagon to carry my dreams. No solutions...just a direction, a way to go.

We left Laguna Beach the next day, and headed East—as our friend Norman said, "to good old Pennsyltucky," where we came from...through the Mojave, gawking at the Canyon, petrified wood, and painted landscape. Thanksgiving in Albuquerque; then racing a cold front home, with the states rolling by like mileposts. A light snow through the Appalachians was only a hint of the fearsome winter that was to batter America for months to come.

We stayed with my parents, sorting our dreams, renewing old relationships and launching the Community Service Foundation. I spent much of my time down in the basement, banging away on my typewriter, filling out government forms, working on this book, and writing presentations, proposals, and an occasional poem:

> *Living in a community*
> *Without geography*
> *Defined by trust*
> *And a cooperative spirit*
>
> *Citizens share*
> *Things*

BEYOND THE SCHOOLHOUSE: Learning In A New Reality

Dreams
And a cosmic view
Of their spaceship Earth

Woman and man
Young and old
In harmony

Feeling and thought
Image and word
In balance

Humanity merges
Into
ONE

Upon hearing this poem, four-year-old Benjamin shouted, "That's us, that's us, that's us!" and ran around the basement, which I report simply as an interested observer.

Frankly, I was not so sure of myself.

Yet, I had a feeling that obsessed me. A feeling that demanded a written expression and a living model of my "dreams" about learning. A feeling that, despite my previous inability to express myself or build such a model, despite my failures, my fumbles and my bumbles, a feeling so clear: that there was still some point in trying again. And again. And again.

I could not verbalize this feeling until I ran across Einstein's *Ideas and Opinions* (1954), and Bucke's Cosmic Consciousness. They confirmed my faith in my own inner vision of truth. Einstein said that even the most creative minds in science were plagued by doubts when "surrounded by a skeptical world," but were guided by a cosmic feeling.

The man who restructured our conception of the universe said, "Only one who has devoted his life to similar ends can have a vivid realization of what has inspired these men and given them the strength to remain true to their purpose in spite of countless failures. It is cosmic religious feeling that gives a man such strength." (Society's growing cosmic feeling demands that we include women in the generalization.)

I am part of a generation touched by a cosmic understanding. If you are uncomfortable relating to it in terms of religion or consciousness, think of it as creative thinking or problem solving. It seems to be an ability to use both halves of the brain simultaneously, or at least interchangeably.

Psychologist Herbert Crovitz in *Galton's Walk* (1970)[66] suggests that we are groping to "find a way to do the same things that we do passively, as in dreaming, while we are awake and with all our wits about us." We are beginning to integrate our conscious and unconscious thinking.

Bucke indicated that this new state of mind gave a person "an enormously greater capacity for learning and initiating," just as self consciousness had been a step beyond simple consciousness.

Carl Sagan's *Dragons of Eden*[67] speculates on the evolution of human intelligence.

"I think the most significant creative activities of our or any other human culture—legal and ethical systems, art and music, science and technology—were made possible only through the collaborative work of the left and right cerebral hemispheres. These creative acts, even if engaged in rarely or only by a few, have changed us and the world. We might say that human culture is the function of the corpus callosum…To solve complex problems in changing circumstances requires the activity of both hemispheres; the path to the future lies through the corpus callosum."

The corpus collosum is the bridge between hemispheres. If human beings have integrated and balanced the left and right brains since the advent of electronic media, a rapid growth of the corpus callosum would have to occur, faster than by evolution.

That capability has been confirmed. In *Scientific American* (February, 1972) Mark Rosensweig, Edward Bennett, and Marian Cleeves Diamond reported on "Brain Changes in Response to Experience,"[68] which showed that rats in a lively environment have more brain growth than rats in a dull setting. The question is: Which is livelier to a human mind; six hours of school, or six hours of television? Think back to your years of elementary school, sitting at a desk most of the day, and you will have the answer. And consider what would happen if children not only watched televisions, but read, sang, listened, daydreamed, built things, performed socially valued services, pursued their strongest interests, created, invented, and problem-solved.

Another study by William Greenbough[69] at the University of Illinois implies that there would be new neural synapses formed by the synthesis of protein and RNA molecules. Still other research indicates that children whose left-brain speech functions are eliminated by brain damage can grow a new speech capability on the right side. Adults cannot, but the flexible capability of a child's brain demonstrates the possibility that children have changed their minds dramatically through years of television viewing.

Whether you accept a right hemispheric feeling or prefer a left hemispheric set of logical proofs, a more advanced human intelligence is now theoretically possible. Further evidence will soon be in hand.[70]

CHAPTER **17**

Age of Genius

Electronic media herald an age of genius.

Since 1946, television has dramatically enhanced human communication and made possible a quantum jump in creative intelligence. That development, however, is blocked by an obstacle established through public law—compulsory schooling.

Do you think the last paragraph is too strong? That's what I thought for a moment after I wrote it. But I looked ahead in my mind at the evidence to be presented and decided to make a stronger statement: Compulsory schooling is crucifying a major advance in human intelligence on a cross of words.

A flow of sounds and images has replaced the alphabet as the fundamental information code of the mind. Television can be transmitted, recorded, stored and retrieved with increasing ease and accessibility. Just as voice, and then print dominated civilization, we have entered a new phase of human experience.

By its nature, television and all digital media are more integrative than any previous human communication medium. The intuitive, visual right hemisphere, long minimized by logical, verbal Western civilization, is now more involved, restoring the balance between the hemispheres of the brain.

Disregarding John Dewey's simplest advice to start where the child is, schools start where the child is not. After years of television viewing, schools try to cram the new student into an alphabet curriculum, like a round peg in a square hole. The consequences are disastrous.

John Debes[71], a pioneer in the visual literacy movement, reports that Robert Thorndike[72], of Columbia University Teacher's College, is guarded in what he has to say about some shocking results from IQ testing. Thorndike's reluctance is easily understood, when we realize that his findings undermine the very institution with which he is associated. What he and his colleagues have discovered is that today's children are more "intelligent" than children forty years ago. In fact, almost all of the improvement can be attributed to nonverbal test items involving visual abstraction ability.

IQ tests, given routinely to students, are based on the assumption that the average "Intelligence Quotient"[73] is 100. The tests were established decades ago, with that average built into them. It is also assumed that a person's IQ will stay fairly constant throughout his life. But IQ tests administered to thousands of people revealed the following:

> A. IQ appears to jump in one-year-olds, at the age when most children begin to watch television.
> B. Two-year-olds' IQs average almost 110, not 100.
> C. Three-, four-, and five-year-olds climb higher.
> D. At five-and-one-half, when the average child enters school, IQ begins to drop steadily.
> E. By eight-and-one-half, when a child is in third or fourth grade, IQ has fallen to 101, close to the old norm of forty years ago.
> Debes wrote, "To what factors can we attribute this remarkable difference between today's child and yesterday's child? There seem to be only one that is so visual and so universal that it could possibly account for the difference: television."

And, I add, to what factors can we attribute this dramatic drop in potential human intelligence? There seems to be only one that is so obsessed with words and so universal that it could possibly account for the loss: school. The IQ gains observed in pre-school children are erased by three years of school, like chalkmarks on a blackboard.[74]

Because IQ tests aim most of their questions toward the verbal left brain, they are underestimating the extent of gain and loss in right-brain intelligence in today's children. A study[75] by Gene Symes at the National Institute for Mental Health more clearly demonstrates the clash between left-brain schools and right-brain kids. He studied third-graders who were having trouble with reading, but without apparent cause.

Starting with 250 youngsters and eliminating anyone who had an older brother or sister with reading problems, whose parents were separated or who seemed to have some other reason for reading difficulty, Symes ended up with fifty boys. After subjecting them to more than seventy different kinds of tests, Symes came to the following conclusion: The boys who had the greatest difficulty with reading in school also had the greatest capacity for three-dimensional visualization. All were markedly inclined toward visual thinking, not words.

Native American Indian culture strongly favors visual communication and thinking. What George Custer said about the Indian in his book *My Life on the Plains*[76], could apply to today's child: "Education, strange as it may appear, seems to weaken rather than strengthen his intellect." School crushes right-brain intelligence like a grape.

In *Popular Photography* (June, 1975), John Debes suggested more visual techniques for schooling, more Sesame Street, more Electric Company. He urged more exposure to photography, more writing using sequences of pictures.

But Josh and Benji, my sons, cannot wait for the unlikely possibility that schools will reform themselves, becoming something else. And children already in the schools have no time to wait for a renaissance. We must eliminate compulsory schooling now, allowing children to escape the school's repressive approach to education. We must encourage less sequential and more visual means to introduce the alphabet and other knowledge to children.

How do children piece together the basic rules of grammar and develop speech without schools? They do so by observing an incredible array of spoken words and by making generalizations in their own minds about how to use them.

A child who says, "I eated the cookie" is simply following the pattern of words that have –ed added to indicate the past tense. The child does not need to be corrected by us. Further observation will make the child aware that the verb "to eat" has a special past tense form—"ate"—and he or she will soon use it properly.

Sesame Street and other new educational television programs use a non-sequential approach to learning, offering programs a variety of visual experiences in random order. They do not teach. They sing, play, joke, tell stories, daydream, get angry, explore, hug, fix things, and laugh. But children learn more, with less anxiety, than in any school I ever saw.

The Associated Press (April 12, 1977) disclosed the results of a federally funded project called the National Assessment of Educational Progress. NAEP compared test profiles of youngsters at 9, 13, and 17 years old[77], covering the last decade.

Not surprisingly, the older students demonstrate what has been called "functional illiteracy," but 9-year-olds "have improved their reading and writing skills in recent years. They can read simple stories and write letters to their friends; they are tolerant of people's cultural differences and believe in an orderly society."

What was incredible to me was not the 9-year-olds' notable progress over their older brothers and sisters. Any parent who has watched their children leaning through Sesame Street and Electric Company and Zoom knows where the gain originated. What was incredible to me was this statement:

"Educators report that it is too soon to say whether these findings mean that the quality of education is definitely improving."

Incredible. Do they really think that schools had anything to do with the improvement? Are educators so blind that they cannot see the positive contributions that television has made?

Or don't they want to see?

Sesame Street was aimed at the pre-school urban child and was launched with great fanfare in urban communities. The Children's Television Workshop made a concerted effort to try to reach urban parents and children, so that kids would watch the new program and parents would get involved in the kids' learning.

The NAEP reports that "black 9-year-olds in particular increased their reading skills from 1971 to 1975." Can anyone believe that the improvement was due to schooling, when millions of federal dollars have been burned in the fires of "educational innovation" during the last two decades, without much discernable effect? And when the school community had the opportunity to produce television programs, the output consisted of dreary stuff with a teacher standing in front of television viewers as if they were in a classroom.

But it is not just the lack of visual media in schools that blocks the advance of the integrated mind fostered by television. The basic obstacle to creative genius is the kind of thinking that schools demand.

William James[78] described genius as a richness of association and a disregard for "old hat." Today's psychologists call that "divergent thinking;" thought that deviates from the norm, that sees associations between things that are not usually associated.[79] Like Isaac Newton seeing the relationship between an apple falling and the concept of gravity.

Schools, on the other hand, encourage "convergent thinking."[80] They want the "right" answer, not an interesting answer. They are not amused by novelty or humor. One is supposed to be a "serious" student. When they ask you a question, they want a normal response: the year, the person, the cause, the reason—not some bizarre association.

If the test asks, "Why did Benjamin Franklin fly a kite in a storm?" the school does not want an answer like, "Because he could not get it to float." Yet a free-floating mind is at the root of discovery and original thought. Archimedes wasn't purposefully pursuing the problem of specific gravity in his laboratory when he shouted, "Eureka!" (I have found it!), but was watching his bathwater spill over the edge of the tub.

The process of analogy, of making comparisons and seeing relationships, requires both hemispheres of the brain working together. While the right brain recognizes patterns that are similar—such as recognizing someone's face—the left brain verifies the pattern, checking logically for discrepancies and exceptions.

If I want to produce an analogy for the modern world's "left-brain domination of the mind," I can generate associations with my right brain, but the most appropriate association will be determined by my left. (Obviously, to put the association into words requires the left brain, as well.)

For example, "left-brain domination of the mind" is like two people sitting on one side of a seesaw, like juggling with one hand, like seeing with one eye, like the sound of one hand clapping, like a rowboat with one oar, like a bicycle with one wheel, or a bicycle with a flat tire. If any of these fits the situation, the left hemisphere will make the determination.

Schools, however, focus mostly on the left brain. They want you to name, choose, match, identify, calculate the answer. They rarely encourage you to create your own answers, to dream, to imagine. Oh, yes...there is "creative" writing, a left-brain communication medium that will be "corrected" and "graded," both left-brain obsessions. But real creative genius is largely stifled.

Genius has always been surrounded by mythological awe. John M. Douglas surveyed the current research on creativity in a two-part article[81] (*Science News*, April 23, 30, 1977) entitled "The Genius of Everyman." He reports: "Now, slowly, this mythology is crumbling before the onslaught of psychological research, which is uncovering the various components of creativity and revealing their potential for development in all of us."

But schools will be the last to act, not because educators are stupid, but because they are blinded by a commitment to an institution and way of learning that is intrinsically uncreative. Their monopoly on education will forestall a golden age in the arts and sciences, and frustrate another generation of children whose round heads were not made to fit into square holes.

Perhaps human intelligence is an iceberg that floats with about ten percent of its mass above water. We have yet to fathom its depths, as we are threatened by our own destructive technology: a minefield of schools and the torpedoes of left-brain prejudice.

Consider the implications of this recent study.[82] Ernesto Spinelli, at the University of Surrey, England, tested people between ages 3 and 35 for their ability to guess hidden cards. In a carefully designed experiment with electronic monitoring to prevent conscious or unconscious fraud, conducting more than 7,500 trials with 700 subjects, Spinelli found these scores:

A. Children between 3.5 and 3.7 scored 762 out of 1500.
B. Children between 4.5 and 4.9 scored 523.
C. Children between 5.0 and 8.0 scored 386.
D. Children over 8 years scored 303.

Perhaps the dramatic drop in this extrasensory ability is due to the cultural belief that there is no such thing as extrasensory, so the children "unlearn" such abilities as they grow older. The fact that children scored 672 when the laws of probability only account for a score of 300 is astounding. The results suggest the existence of a higher intelligence in humans than we have dared expect.[83]

Until our left brain balances our right, the evidence of potential intelligence will accumulate like murder clues, with very reputable detectives providing the data. When our logical civilization is exposed as the culprit, compulsory schooling will prove to be the murder weapon in the slaying of an age of genius.

CHAPTER **18**

Seeing the Forest

Late last night, I decided to reread everything I had written so far on this book, out loud. I wanted to see if my words were "ringing true," and to make sure that I wasn't writing down any more words than I could stand to say.

At about five o'clock, I emerged from my basement like a bug from under a rock. I had seen a hint of light outside and decided to greet the morning. Upstairs, I flicked on the remote control of my parents' big color television. The screen dawned instantly with a gray blizzard. Scanning the channels, I sensed an absence and realized that New York had disappeared from the air.

Sure enough. I finally found NBC 4, operating on independent power, and was made aware of a massive blackout;[84] the second in twelve years. As I watched the informal newscast from the newsroom, I felt a strong sense of the hooked-together-simultaneousness of live television that makes you feel involved-in-what's-happening, even though it may be a hundred miles away.

And something else. I got the distinct feeling that some people were pleased or fascinated by the abrupt shutdown of modern metropolis. Not just looters, but the cleaning woman who walked down 82 stories and found herself "on the air" as television news. Or the suburbanite who got an extra day off.

A videotape of Brooklyn streets: some looted stores; crowds; quieter streets; and suddenly, in the middle of the summer darkness…candle lights, tables, laughter, celebration…the clientele and bartender of a local liquor establishment had moved themselves—iced beer, glasses, ashtrays and all—right out there on the street, as if it were a Paris café.

Inside behemoth buildings, little people climbed and descended infinite steps, huffing and puffing, while an NBC employee spent the night walking to the newsroom from Newark through the Holland Tunnel. An Iowa woman shared her feelings about coming to Manhattan with her parents that day, finding themselves in a blackened Radio City Music Hall, thinking it was part of the show.

When the lights go out, a lot of barriers fall. Rich and poor come together in odd circumstances. It is very difficult to stand on ceremony when you're trapped inside an elevator. Unfortunately, the barriers go back up when the lights go on again. New York resumes its breathless pace. But I have the strangest notion that many would like to pull the plug more often.

In the Bronx, where I had lived as a small boy, many white ethnic neighborhoods are now Black and Hispanic. Little girls and boys watch television in apartments like I did in the late 1940s, but there is a big difference between then and now, them and me. I soon moved from the city to the suburbs, from the concrete to the grass and trees, from the urban scene to a new way of life. The chances of that happening to the kids in those aging buildings are very slim. The dreams that television explodes in their heads will tempt them, but that's all. As they grow up, most will bang into the brick wall of their limited opportunity and recognize that in terms of achieving "success," they have a better chance of being struck by lightning.

The American Dream Machine just isn't what it used to be.

Children As People | chapter 19

Social mobility is much tougher when an aging industrial giant cannot produce enough jobs. And many of the jobs are nothing to boast about. Not just for poor folks, but for the kids with the golden future, who went to college and played the game to win. Suicide among young people has increased 250 percent since 1950 and keeps climbing, as potential cosmic kids find life too grim to live.

Those who watched the looting unleashed by the blackout and cursed "the niggers" and "the spics"—like some separate human species—don't seem to understand. We are all in the boat and will sink or float together: The ruined merchant and his jobless employees, the old Yiddish grandma who gets splattered across the pavement by callous punks, the black newspaper vendor who has been robbed forty times, the salesman who is pulled from his car and beaten to a pulp, the first-grader who is jeered by angry whites protesting integration, the second-grader who is hustled by the neighborhood gang, the rape victim who is accused of seduction, the innocent youth who is smacked around by angry cops, the fireman who stops a bullet while trying to stop the flames.

It's madness all around and there's nowhere to point the finger. It's us. You and me, everybody. We are all part of the same, indivisible life force that rules the universe. No exceptions. Nobody gets left out by nature, just by each other. People drawing lines between people.

Let those who see the world as bits and pieces show us where on the surface of the earth the gods drew the boundary for Mexico. Let them show us which shade of skin darkness designates when you are "black" and when you are "white," and where in the stars the supremacy of the "white race" is written. Let them explain why a woman should earn less than a man doing similar work. Let them show us college graduates and congressmen who don't sweat like factory workers and farmers. Let them define the reasons why a V.I.P. is more important than you or me.

As long as we let the left brain dominate civilization, we will only see the trees, never the forest, never the unifying wholeness that has been proclaimed by every religious giant from Christ to Buddha, from Mohammed to Lao Tsu. We are One. And in the words of the ancient Shemah, the Hebrew phrase that every Jew commits to memory and is supposed to say with his or her last dying breath, "Hear, oh Israel, the Lord our God, the Lord is One."

We are on a common journey, together, all of us. Every human being on the planet shares the biosphere of Earth. When we invent categories with our left brain, we divide the unity of our existence. Something goes wrong when young people are treated as second-class citizens. Something is unnatural about dividing learning from life and calling it "education," and putting it in special buildings called "schools."

The rise of the cosmic mind offers an alternative to the fragmentation of the self-conscious mind, which has dominated human life as long as anyone can remember. We can now climb the mountain and look across the diversity of trees that have characterized human experience, and see the wholeness of the green forest that surrounds us. And then we will notice how we can modify our technology, adjust our society, and curb our material greed to restore balance.

Not a new social program, not another military campaign, not a miraculous invention will resolve our plight. Just the quiet harmony of individuals working together, unified by a new, integrated mind.

CHAPTER **19**

Children As People

"You're just teasing me," Josh insisted.

"I'm not teasing, Josh. There's a law, everywhere in the United States, that children can't vote."

"I know you're teasing me."

I was getting a little angry with my five-year-old.

"I'm not kidding, Josh. You can't vote, not until you're eighteen. I wouldn't kid you about that. I'm serious."

Finally, I could see that he believed me, but he wasn't very happy about it. I had been talking about the upcoming election with him, and it did not occur to me that he thought he could vote. He's had an interest in politics since the impeachment hearings on television, and had often asked questions about what was going on, but for some reason the existence of age requirements for voting had gone unmentioned.

"Why can't I vote?"

I hesitated. The truth was that he probably was no less informed about the candidates than many adults who would mindlessly pull the straight party lever and guess at the ballot questions.

"You can't vote because most people think that you have to be older to know what's going on. I'm not sure that I agree with that, but that's the way it is, and you'll just have to accept the situation. Besides, you're not tall enough to reach the levers in the voting machine."

The latter part of my explanation seemed to satisfy him most, and he went on his way, leaving me pondering the issue he had raised. I had thought about similar issues before. I have seen so many instances when he behaved in a more careful or responsible manner than many adults. I have begun to realize that maturity is more a matter of attitude than age.

John Holt[85], in his book *Escape From Childhood* (1974), points out that the institution of childhood did not exist several hundred years ago. Although children have been controlled by adults as long as there have been little people, the distinct segregation from "adulthood" that characterizes modern life did not begin to appear until the 1600s.

Centuries ago, children were given important responsibility when they were very small, and they achieved full independence at a much younger age than now. They married, owned property, even ruled empires before their teens. But just as modern civilization created categories to put adults into, it created a special category for youth.

Children are now the least free people in the world. They are more oppressed than the most unfortunate racial or religious minority. Holt compiled a list of rights that children lack:

> The right to equal treatment before the law
> The right to vote
> The right to be legally responsible for one's life and acts
> The right to work for money
> The right to privacy
> The right to financial independence
> The right to direct one's own education
> The right to travel and live away from home

> The right to receive minimum income from the state
> The right to seek and choose guardians other than one's parents
> And the right to do, in general, what any adult may legally do.

Children are totally at the mercy and whim of adults. Adults can make them work for free, hit them, force their affections on them, dress them in silly clothes, whistle for them like dogs, strip them naked, humiliate them, tease them, trick them, take their money, and—of course—force them to go to school.

The young person of seventeen has a few more rights than a baby, such as the right to drive an automobile. But there are no legal definitions that gradually increase a child's rights with age or demonstrated responsibility. It's pretty much all at age eighteen, and nothing until then.

In a recent national survey conducted for the Senate subcommittee on child and human development, it was revealed that violence toward children in America is pervasive. Based on what parents were willing to admit in an interview, the survey estimates that besides millions who are spanked, slapped, shoved, hit with an object, or punched, between 1 and 1.4 million children in the United States between ages 3 and 17 have been threatened with a knife or gun.

To the average middle class parent, like myself, hitting a child for "disciplinary" reasons has always been acceptable. Yet when I began to examine my behavior I realized that I hit my children out of anger more than reason. And since I have begun to change my behavior, I realize how unjust my previous position was.

I never allowed my children to hit me when I was unfair or irresponsible, and I would never treat or talk to adults the way I treated and talked to them. Although I prided myself on my serious chats with them about all sorts of knowledge, I was a blatant hypocrite in other matters.

We are all learners in life, and I am learning lessons from my children. They are showing me a new way of dealing with people and that the rights of children are intimately related to everyone's rights. Abraham Lincoln said that we "cannot endure permanently half-slave and half-free." The indignities we impose on children are reflected in the indignities we impose on each other when we grow up. If we don't deal with the rights of children, we can never be truly free.

As a parent, I always felt that I imposed things on my children "for their own good." Since I have reexamined my actions and motives carefully, I have to admit that I was more often imposing my own prejudices, doubts, fears, insecurities, and desires. For example, the matter of creativity.

Silvano Arieti,[86] one of America's more prominent psychiatrists, wrote in *Creativity: The Magic Synthesis* (1976):[87]

"Clinical observations disclose that most parents, although believing that they help children in fostering creativity, actually do not do so. On closer examination, we realize that they do not practice what they believe; they have good intentions, but they give wrong directions. Many parents show inhibiting anxieties, such as worrying whether their children appear unusual, introverted, peculiar. They are more concerned with external success and popularity than with inner growth and creativity...most parents first of all want to make sure their children, once grown up, will be self-supporting."

But on their parents' terms.

As for teachers, Arieti reports that E. Paul Torrance,[88] in *Education and the Creative Potential*,[89] said they are responsible for hindering creative thinking through "premature attempts to eliminate fantasy; restrictions on manipulativeness and curiosity; overemphasis or misplaced emphasis on sex roles; overemphasis on prevention, fear and timidity; misplaced emphasis on certain verbal skills; emphasis on destructive criticism."

Unfortunately, our paternalism has backfired. The recent upsurge of youth crime, especially in urban areas where young toughs mercilessly rob and kill aged people for pocket money, cannot be dealt with because the law keeps children from accepting responsibility for their own crimes. And those adults who want to eliminate these special privileges of children in the courts do not want to give them any reciprocal rights or responsibilities. They don't see that our extensive restrictions on young people are often the source of their hostility and violence.

During my last months as media coordinator in a public school district, I was involved with kids from a group home for juvenile offenders and some "bad" students from the high school, who had combined efforts to produce a multi-screen slide and film program. The day before the presentation, the boys from the high school received a week of "detention" as punishment for my inadvertent failure to notify their teacher that they were helping me to set up.

Although I tried to remedy the problem with an apology, it took two meetings and a threat to take the matter to the school board before the punishment was revoked. No one had been interested in hearing out the students before the sentencing; a basic right for any adult. What should have been a small dream fulfilled, turned into another nightmare. I submitted my resignation a few weeks later.

I could relate a hundred instances concerning violations of children's rights in schools, naming teachers and principals, but I am not interested in trying to humiliate people. I merely suggest that we take a good, hard look at what we call "discipline," and consider whether the same behavior directed toward adults would not be called "injustice."

Children grow up to be adults eventually, and they tend to treat their children as they have been treated. We are entangled in a vicious cycle that we must break.

I have heard teachers in faculty rooms, talking about individual children as if privacy and reputation were meaningless, as if they were less perfect than teachers. How did we ever get to such a ridiculous state of affairs?

I don't know for sure, but I think it has something to do with building institutions in which the consumer of the product has no right to refuse it, no right to evaluate it...no rights at all.

CHAPTER **20**

Life As Learning

I could see it all atop Coney Island. From frothy-surfed sand to cloud-shrouded skyscrapers. The Big Town, on a magic carpet above the boardwalk. Slender strands and whirring machinery, higher and higher, while the parachute above me hung limp.

Across town, the 1964 World's Fair[90] and its Unisphere proclaimed "Peace and Understanding," while steamy Vietnam jungles thundered with a war of misunderstanding. A quarter-century earlier, my parents' generation thronged Flushing Meadows to see television and highways of "The World of Tomorrow,"[91] but soon man-made lightning in Steinmetz Hall presaged man-made hell in Poland.

Suspended from the giant tower, a transplanted antique of that not-so-long-ago World's Fair, one could sense the incredible jump that a generation made in a lifetime. The fading tramp and trenches of Europe and the crackle of radio, the luck of Lindy and the hard times of the Depression, my dad in the Philippines and my mom crying over people's letters in the Office of Censorship. Millions merged in conflict and explored the far reaches of human horror, endlessly extended from World War to Cold War.

The parents of the postwar wanted to give their children what they had lacked: security and permanent prosperity. They built the World's Fair dream of 1939. Constrained by the limits of industrialism, their magic carpet has become an electric blanket, fast running out of extension cords and cheap energy.

"The torch has passed to a new generation," said John F. Kennedy, and so it will again. There is no such thing as life without risk, as my parents and their peers well know, but seem to forget. Life demands change without warning. When a particular journey reaches its zenith, you just have to let go and...free fall.

Free fall with the Earth rushing up on you, a jolt to boredom, routine, ruts, and vested interest. Alfred North Whitehead[92] wrote that all major advances in civilization wreck the societies in which they occur. Institutions are not permanent. Free fall. That's what life requires, and that's what is required of learning. Learning that follows life without constraint. Learning that merges with life and moves with it. Learning that billows like a parachute and brings us softly to Mother Earth.

The Coney Island parachute jump[93] is now extinct, but not the dream that built it. Unlike the decayed giant, the dream of my parents' generation has spawned a living heir to carry the torch of human aspiration. And they really have no choice but to trust in their children's vision: a new magic carpet with a new kind of energy.

Synergy. The energy of the whole, of complete round entities, of balanced systems, of integrated minds:

ENERGY = energy + energy + SYNERGY

The energy of a whole system is greater than the total energy of its individual components. The power of people working together is far greater than the power of people working apart. Synergy is the fruit of cooperation.

The Last Whole Earth Catalog (1971)[94] and subsequent *Whole Earth Epilog* (1974), books dealing with tools for alternative lifestyles, have sold by the millions to postwar kids. The purpose of

the volumes is clearly stated, resolving the right hemispheric search for lost gods:
"We are as gods, and might as well get good at it."
This might include losing the pride that went before the fall we are in the process of taking. Rolling with such a fall is our present lesson...a realm of personal power is developing—power of the individual to conduct his own education, find his own inspiration, shape his own environment, and share his adventure with whomever is interested.

That is the purpose of the Community Service Foundation:[95] To provide a vehicle for individuals who wish to shape their environment and realize that there is no curriculum, no course of study, no school to teach us how. As Aristotle put it:
"That which we must learn to do, we learn by doing."
And so it has been with us, learning by doing. Susan and I have explored every opportunity, from trite to obscure, unlikely to imminent, and have settled on developing model learning programs for young people. The bits and pieces approach of schools is obviously unsatisfactory. Schools are old tools failing at a new task. They frustrate a human intelligence that rejects assembly line learning. Schools separate preparation and practice, but a new age requires direct experience.

People learn by experience and only a few of those experiences occur in schools. Most of the really important ones, those that deal with the day-to-day business of living, do not. They are a fundamental part of life itself. Learning to survive in a changing world is now our life's work.

The Community Service Foundation's model of learning is on the verge of becoming operational. Still somewhat undefined, we are gathering together a community of learners who can demonstrate a viable alternative to compulsory schooling.[96]

The pace has been slow, with the web of red tape that government spins, and my own feelings that haste should be avoided. As I complete

BEYOND THE SCHOOLHOUSE: Learning In A New Reality

each of these chapters, I feel clearer about the specifics of our enterprise, and the dream seems to gather momentum in my mind.

The purpose of education, as best I can discern, is not preparation for life, but something else. The purpose of education is to be life itself. Every split-second of our existence is our learning, and the sum total of our learning is our life.

When I scan the images of my past, I remember school as a room with a portrait of George Washington, a flag, the world's slowest clock, blackboards, desks, and windows through which my daydreams wandered. Monotones of school pale beside the carnival of life.

Bumping into barracuda in the clear Caribbean and racing a rainstorm down a Maine mountain. Holding the earplugs of a dead man in the depths of a zinc mine and holding my ears like a deaf man in the wake of a blast. Cooking gallons of Italian for spaghetti night at Al and Larry's Saloon, and hauling trees for a three-story bonfire.

Sealing socks in plastic packages, mindless motion of human machines, boxes in boxes, cartons in cases, losing myself in contest with the clock. Sneaking a ride of ball bearing speed, losing myself on the curve of the conveyor.

Cleaning toilets in my father's factory, learning humility. Driving his delivery truck and singing folk songs to Willamsport, without a radio. Driving camp kids back to the Bronx at rush hour, with a vomit bag in the glove compartment. Driving a box lunch truck with pineapple upside-down cakes for the Tidy Didy lady, and coffee for Bethlehem Steel. Chauffeuring the current president of the Dominican Republic in a big Caddy limousine, hearing tales of the fall of Trujillo.

Selling lemonade from the neighborhood's first cardboard lemonade machine, printing a homemade three-color magazine with traced cartoons, taping my own disc jockey programs on an early Webcor with a blinking green eye. Staging magic shows and movie matinees and running a phone line with the kids next door, chatting when Bob got up for his paper route.

And every book and movie and TV program and comic book and song and symphony and poem that I ever heard or read or played or ended up tucking away for another day.

And every business venture, from island trips for college kids to renting filmstrips to schools. Failures were the best of all: rough on the ego, but laden with learning. The School of Hard Knocks outranks Harvard.

Schools make failure seem evil, like something you should not do. A permanent scar on your permanent record, only to be redeemed by waves of "A's." Speaking strictly for myself, failure has been my wisest tutor, and I have spent many productive hours at its knee.

Schools are the dullest event in life's fair. They rule out anything they cannot control or measure. But risk is the rollercoaster of life, and direct, purposeful experience is the vehicle that carries us to its highest peaks, where we sense the adventure and opportunity around us.

BEYOND THE SCHOOLHOUSE: Learning In A New Reality

PART **THREE**

Learning By Experience

A knowledge not gained by words but by touch, sight, sound, victories, failures, sleeplessness, devotion, love—the human experiences and emotions of this earth and of oneself and other men; and perhaps, too, a little faith, and a little reverence for things you cannot see.

– Adlai Stevenson, 1954[97]

BEYOND THE SCHOOLHOUSE: Learning In A New Reality

CHAPTER **21**

Things You Cannot See

"Dad, would you lift me up there?"

I was already lying on the grass when Josh decided to climb a tree. "Can't you get up yourself?"

"It's too high."

"Okay, okay." Then I settled back down, soaking up sunshine.

"Hey, Dad, look! An 'L.'"

"Right on, Benj." He was holding up a broken twig.

"Hey, Dad, look. A '7.'"

"All right, Benj."

Next a V, then another break in the twig, an N.

"Hey, Dad, look. A 'Z.'"

Giving up hope of facing the sun, I changed spots, moving to Benji's twig pile in the shade of the tree.

"You know what, Dad?"

"What, Benj?"

"Hey, Dad," dropped a voice from above.

"Yes, Josh."

"I'm going around the tree for a second time."

I smiled up

"You know what, Dad?"

"What, Benj?"

"Joshie looks like a windmill, the way he goes around the tree."

"Yeah, he does."

"Or a helicopter. Look, a 'W.'"

Josh swung out of the tree like a monkey scrambling for sticks.

"I'm gonna make an 'O.'"

"Good, Josh."

"And a 'Q.'"

"Yeah."

"Hey, Dad?"

"What, Benj?"

"What kind of tree is this?"

Josh looked up, too. I hesitated.

"I'm not sure. Well, it's a maple. Like the trees next to Grandma and Grandpa's house. Aha! Come over here and I can show you what kind of maple."

I walked into the sunlight and they followed.

"Look at the tree. Doesn't it look silver, the way the sunlight hits the leaves? That's why it's called a silver maple."

"Yeah, it does. It does look silver."

"Hey, whaddayaknow?" A silver maple," Benji clowned.

Back in the shade, Benji wanted to try tree climbing, but lost his nerve in the branches.

"I think I'll come down now," he said, trying to be casual about it.

While I brought him down, Josh climbed back up without my assistance, flashing a broad smile of self-satisfaction. Benji went back to his twigs and sticks.

"Benji, I don't think we can put all those sticks in the van when we leave. Why don't you narrow your pile down to two or three favorite sticks?"

What had started as one's "sword" earlier in the afternoon had become an arsenal, as we wandered around the college campus. Josh and Benj staged scenes from Star Wars, Batman, and an unknown source that Benji was imitating when he climbed atop a brick post, sword raised high, and confronted an advancing passerby with his challenge, "Stand a'guard!"

Faltering at the sight of the midget swordsman, the passerby smiled and went on his way. Benji tried that approach several more times, until it became clear that no one else was wearing a sword today. Now he selected his prize sticks and we all walked toward the van.

"You know, Dad, those barbell things must have been heavy."

"What 'barbell things,' Josh?"

"Can I unlock the door?"

"Sure. Here are the keys."

We stored Josh and Benji's sticks carefully.

"You know, those barbell things that the workmen were carrying?"

He could see my puzzled look.

"When we were sitting outside the bathroom waiting for Benji. Those workmen came past us with the barbell things. Like at movie theaters."

I flashed back on the scene. Maintenance workers had been carrying some post-and-chain stands, used to form lines at movie theaters and such.

"Oh, I see what you mean. I'll bet they were heavy."

I started up the engine.

"Hey, Dad. David lives a few blocks back that way, doesn't he?"

"That's right, Josh."

"And my camp's down there," said Benji, pointing down the hill.

"Yup. Wanna drive by?"

"Of course." And off we went.

I don't pretend to understand the details of human intelligence, but its broadcast outlines are becoming apparent.

This afternoon's experiences illustrate the process as accurately as I can record them. Human intelligence seems to be a process of analogy-making, of finding similarities, of comparing and contrasting, of understanding new by assimilating with old. It seems to occur without chronology or sequence, without external evaluation. It seems to occur within a framework that you cannot see or count or measure, but that exists like the roots and branches of a tree, constantly expanding in new directions. It seems to transcend the narrow boundaries of school learning and the fumbling attempts of adults to manage it.

The role of adults in a child's development, it seems to me, is to facilitate a natural process by exposing a kid to lots of things and happenings, and by imposing authority only where health, safety, courtesy or common sense require.

A child's growth seems to falter in the presence of adults who always impose themselves on children. I have watched my sons, particularly younger Benjamin, clam up like a shellfish when a strong-willed adult descends on them. Josh deals with such situations more successfully, but Benji never had the intense adult attention directed toward a first child and grandchild.

I have a lot of faith in my children's ability to sort out the universe, possibly in ways beyond my comprehension. J. Robert Oppenheimer said: "There are children playing in the street who could solve some of my top problems in physics, because they have modes of sensory perception that I lost long ago."

And I have a strong notion that schools play a great part in destroying those modes of sensory perception. Not just schools, of course, but the cynicism of the adult world in general. Maybe that's what Jesus meant when he said that unless we turned and became as little children, we would in no way enter the kingdom of Heaven.[98]

Maria Montessori[99] suggested that the defect in our way of dealing with children would continue passing from generation to generation, until we came to grips with the problem. The problem, as I interpret it, is that we don't trust children. We don't trust their inner vision and their ability to make important decisions by themselves. We perpetuate their lack of responsibility and lament their failures of responsibility when they occur.

People of all ages need varied experiences of their own choosing. Risk and consequence are essential to growth. Security and paternalism are essential to stagnation.

We must resist the narrow definition of intelligence arrogantly thrust upon children by schools, for educators are stumbling in the darkness of ignorance. The revelations of scientific research are shaking the traditional tree of knowledge as we discover the diverse patterns that human minds may follow in learning and communication.

Today (July 23, 1977), an Associated Press story from San Diego further confirms our need for a broader conception of intelligence:

"Grace and Virginia Kennedy, 6-year-old identical twins who were regarded as severely retarded for most of their lives,[100] are actually bright children who invented their own private language... Researchers said that the girls know four languages. They understand English and German with good comprehension, although they do not speak either one. In addition to their private language, the girls have learned sign language as part of their therapy."

"The hospital said this week that investigators now know that Grace calls Virginia 'Cabengo,' while Virginia called Grace 'Poto.' The rest of their speech is still a mystery to outsiders."

Schools are simply too inflexible to respond to the creative potential of humanity. Vested interest and myopia dominate the school monopoly in education. We need a new spirit of adventure and experimentation to carry us beyond the schoolhouse.

Alex F. Osborn,[101] inventor of "the brainstorming principle,"[102] suggested that creative ideas require an environment which postpones criticism. Imagination is stifled by premature scrutiny. When I have tried to outline my ideas, most listeners have pounced on me with logical objections even before the whole scheme was revealed. They never subject the school establishment to the same questioning. The difficulties of starting a new model of learning from scratch require a certain tolerance and "suspended judgment," so that a new bird can at least get off the ground.

I have established the Community Service Foundation as a state-licensed academic institution, which will meet the requirements of school attendance laws. I intend to gradually expand its scope to a wide variety of learners who can benefit from direct, purposeful experience rather than classroom learning.

If my idea seems vague, that is because it is based in things you cannot see: not curriculum and textbooks, but an abiding faith in the curiosity and goodness of children of all ages.

CHAPTER **22**

Reality

On a hot, June day a century ago, George Armstrong Custer[103] and his Seventh Cavalry met destiny on a grassy knoll overlooking the Little Bighorn River. Dreams of conquest and glory quickly faded before the unblinking stare of reality. But the reality of history is no more certain than the reality of the present. That which we believe to be true is always subject to question.

One hundred years after the bluecoats' defeat, Thomas B. Marquis'[104] book shook historical reality. Disputing the prevailing belief that Custer and his soldiers valiantly fought to the last man, Marquis argued that the terrified mortals who found themselves in a hopeless situation did what hopeless people often do: Custer and his beleaguered troops collectively committed suicide.

It does not matter whether you agree with the book, *Keep the Last Bullet for Yourself* (1976),[105] or not. Its very existence suggests the possibility of another reality. And that is what I am doing through this book: suggesting the possibility of another reality.

Social reality is the prevailing truth in any society. Members of society collectively share a view of reality, enforced by vested interest or habit, consciously or unconsciously; they believe the same basic beliefs. This shared reality is fundamental to successful groups of all sizes. Without general agreement on some level, groups cannot function. Clubs, associations, and societies all unravel when they fail to maintain a consensus of truth among their members.

And when members of a group do not share reality, conflict occurs. In our society, conflict takes the form of anxiety, violence, crime, drug addiction, divorce, emotional disturbance. Simple arithmetic indicates that a growing number of people do not accept the prevailing reality and express themselves in a wide variety of anti-social behavior. Insanity, pill-popping, looting, heroin, murder, prostitution, psychosomatic illness, child-beating, rape, truancy, alcoholism; all occur when people no longer believe they can fulfill their needs within the framework of our social reality. They try to meet their needs through irresponsible, unrealistic and often cruel behavior.

I am no exception. I have behaved in unrealistic and irresponsible ways on more occasions than I care to remember. I have also been told by fellow educators that I was "too idealistic." Some friends and relatives have said that I should consider treatment by a psychiatrist. And I have considered it, but I decided to follow the advice of those who feel the best path to reality is to be one's own psychiatrist.

Unhappy with America's reality and constantly dreaming of something else, I found *Reality Therapy: A New Approach to Psychiatry* (1965),[106] an appropriate tool in my rehabilitation.

Psychiatrist William Glasser[107] challenged his profession when his book appeared. He said that it is a waste of time to sit around and psychoanalyze dreams and personal history. All mental illness represents an inability to fulfill one's needs responsibly. The therapist must help the emotionally disturbed to face the "moral consequences" of irresponsible behavior and to begin to replace it with realistic, responsible action.

My own irresponsible behavior took many forms: excessive anger and bitterness, deteriorating concern with my appearance, cigarette chain-smoking, selfish obsession with my own problems, overeating, difficulty getting out of bed on workdays, lack of understanding for Susan and our sons, and more.

I have searched my soul, determined to root out my irresponsibility. I let myself smile more, smoke less, stay cool, take an interest in others, get into my family, and I have—with varying degrees of success—accomplished reform. But I cannot stop dreaming and feeling that something else is at the root of my unhappiness and the unhappiness of many others.

I decided to follow the advice of Carl Jung, whose patients tried to resolve their conflicts by creative endeavor. And that is what brings me to this writing, and to the suggestion that there is another reality...a natural reality that underlies social reality. The reality of realities.

Like Custer, whose arrogant dream of superiority and glory caused him to march foolishly against too many Indians, our whole civilization is foolishly marching against Mother Nature, who will not be fooled.

I walked through an airport late one night, and realized I was walking through the skeleton of an industrial age dinosaur. Many thousands of square feet of floor space, many millions of cubic feet of air space, then serving less than fifty people. Air conditioners throbbing, fluorescent lights humming, escalators rolling, display cabinets boasting dreams of greed.

Madness.

Is it sane to believe that we can forever live like pigs, knee-deep in garbage, slopping away the Earth's precious treasures?

Glasser said that irresponsible behavior occurs when the individual pursues short-term gain against the long-term reality. Thinking that his irresponsible behavior will fulfill his needs, the individual finds that the problem gets worse.

BEYOND THE SCHOOLHOUSE: Learning In A New Reality

And so it goes with modern civilization—mad with power and possession—grabbing the latest gadgets and goodies like children running wild in a toy store, living as if tomorrow never comes. Our society desperately needs reality therapy.

I am not naïve. I do not feel that a magic fairy will wave away our troubles and I have no illusions about changing the whole world by myself, but I can change a piece of it. I can make constructive changes in myself and perhaps in my community.

Back from California, I went to speak with administrators at my old school district. Our meeting was cordial and I tried to explain my ideas concerning a program of direct experience for kids who were most troublesome to them, so-called "discipline" problems.

When I told them that the Community Service Foundation would try to interest young people in meaningful ecology projects like greenhouse intensive gardens, methane gas generators, and fish farming, several laughed and one howled shrilly, "Fish farming!" as if I had just delivered Johnny Carson's funniest punchline.

I drove away from the meeting and gazed at the complex of brick and mortar. It included the new high school (completed in time for my last year as media coordinator), a junior high, another high school, and an administration building. The operating costs for those real estate dreams had surpassed anyone's wildest nightmare. What was so funny about ecology?

A few rows of evergreens on the windy northwest sides of each building and some solar-assist heating wouldn't tickle anyone's funny bone. Nor is fish farming a joking matter. A few weeks after our meeting, another stretch of the Massachusetts coast was closed to fishing because of toxic pollution. Where will we get our fish after we have destroyed their natural habitat?

Among the Sioux, there was no distinction between social and natural reality. The sun, stars, seasons, animals, rivers, land and weather merged with human existence. Knowledge and interpretation of natural forces was the science and religion of life. Imagine the horror in Sioux hearts, as they watched the extermination of the buffalo by white invaders who seemed to view nature as an enemy to be conquered.

When we build houses without the slightest regard for the position of sun and trees, when we dump new chemicals into flesh and soil without understanding their ultimate effects, when we produce so many spray cans that their gases alter the biosphere, we are demonstrating the unrealistic contempt for nature that has characterized our civilization for centuries and will prove to be its undoing.

Jean Jacques Rousseau, whose writings are pillars in the development of modern democracy, also produced an important work on education. Published in the 1700s, Rousseau's *Emile*[108] described the self-education of a young man, and warned that humanity should live with reverence for nature. Two centuries later, his warning is still appropriate, only more so.

As I resolve my personal conflicts by expressing my dreams on paper, I hope that I can suggest a more natural reality in education.

J.A. Hadfield points out that suggestion "does not consist in making an individual believe what is not true: suggestion consists in making something come true by making him believe in its possibility."[109]

BEYOND THE SCHOOLHOUSE: Learning In A New Reality

CHAPTER 23

The Revolution

Every day, the sun dawns on a slightly altered planet. Each revolution of the Earth brings change, and the day may come when all that remains of humanity is a thin line in the wall of a new Grand Canyon. Or perhaps we will outlast the stars of our galaxy. We simply do not know.

The freshness of morning reminds us that we all have one-way tickets, and that no one has been this way before. Life is unprecedented. Our destination is only a guess or a dream, and the resurgence of the right brain in the human species is just another change in a process of infinite revolution that spins us through the universe.

George Gallup III,[110] the pollster, believes that we "may be in the early stage of a profound religious revival." And historian William Irwin Thompson,[111] in *At the Edge of History*,[112] predicts that, "by 1984, we should be at a fork in the road. Then everyone should be able to see clearly the choice to be made. One road will lead toward nuclear power, strip mining, and authoritarian governments that can underwrite the workers' pension fund and protect society from revolution and terrorism. The other road will lead toward a religious awakening on the level of the great universal religions...a change of heart and mind, a wedding of nature and culture, a new kind of community that expresses the sacredness of Earth."

Inventor Buckminster Fuller[113] said that change is fundamental to religion, "for God, to me, it seems, is a verb, not a noun." And in *No More Secondhand God* (1963),[114] he predicted the natural occurrence of a new religious era, during which humanity no longer swallows secondhand knowledge, but pursues direct experience:

> *The revolution has come —*
> *set on fire from the top.*
> *Let it burn swiftly.*
> *Neither the branches, trunk nor roots*
> *Will be endangered.*
> *Only last year's leaves and*
> *The parasite-bearded moss and orchids*
> *will not be there*
> *when the next spring brings fresh growth*
> *and free standing flowers.*

Francis Fitzgerald,[115] in her Pulitzer prize-winning *Fire In The Lake* (1972),[116] pointed out the difference between Oriental and Western concepts of revolution. "Revolution for Westerners is an abrupt reversal in the order of society, a violent break with history. But the Vietnamese...for them revolution was a natural and necessary event within the historical cycle."

As written in the ancient Chinese *I Ching*:[117] "Times change and with them, their demands. Thus the seasons change in the course of a year. In the world cycle, there are spring and autumn in the life of peoples and nations, and these call for social transformations."

And the Beatles, in their hit song "Revolution," differed with violent radicals and saw change as spiritual growth. "But when you talk about destruction, don't you know that you can count me out… You tell me it's the institution. Well, you know, you better free your mind instead."

The religious and mystical right brain is influencing the changes we are experiencing. Even violence has taken on the trappings of the occult and satanic. But the underlying possibilities seem healthy and positive; an ecological spirit, a renewed appreciation for nature, a harmony among living things.

The revolution is not utopian. Life cannot be perfect. Conflict and catastrophe will still exist. But the nature of human conflict can shift from violence to argument; from destruction to decision. People can learn to deal more effectively with their emotions; we are potentially more peaceful.

The revolution will not involve people changing other people. Only they individual can change her- or himself. We can, however, change the environment. Our golden age rests on the growth of a new human environment, which minimizes conflict and encourages cooperation, which stimulates creativity rather than confining and stifling it.

We are the revolution; the revolution is us. And though we cannot be sure of our future, as surely as the world turns, a new reality will greet the light of day.

BEYOND THE SCHOOLHOUSE: Learning In A New Reality

CHAPTER **24**

Learning Systems

"A Learning System has as its purpose to bring people into contact with resources for learning." Kenneth Silber (*Audiovisual Instruction*, September, 1972) contrasted "The Learning System"[118] philosophy with that of the current educational system.

Schools treat people as if they are basically evil, and need to be controlled to fit into society, but the learning system assumes their basic goodness and desire to learn. Schools assume that an individual cannot learn on his or her own, but must be taught by a group of professionals who decide what the person may learn. The learning system regards the individual as the best judge of his or her own learning. Knowledge is not the special property of teachers, but is available to all, much of it through daily interaction with the social environment.

The educational system is closed and opposing philosophies are not tolerated, violating fundamental democratic principles. The learning system is open, with opposing philosophies an integral part of its operation. In the comprehensive, city-wide learning system that Silber proposed, structured schools are one of the choices available to the learner.

BEYOND THE SCHOOLHOUSE: Learning In A New Reality

My objection to Silber's comprehensive Learning System is not based on its philosophy, but on its implications. A tax-funded learning system will spawn another monstrous bureaucracy, like the present school establishment. My feeling is that we should view life itself as the comprehensive learning system and allow a diversity of public and private learning systems to function simultaneously.

Though no longer compulsory, public schools initially would be the most popular choice among learning systems. With tradition and fear of the unknown keeping the less adventurous from trying other approaches to learning, the schools have a decided advantage. However, faced with real competition, the schools may deal with some of the most obvious defects now protected by monopoly. Many of the assets of the public schools would be opened to more extensive use by individuals and groups: libraries, film collections, television studios, gymnasiums, swimming pools, auditoriums.

Sharing public school resources and facilities with other schools and adult learners already occurs in many communities, especially those that open the schools in the evening for general use. In Pennsylvania, free daily transportation is provided for resident children who attend non-public schools within ten miles of their public school district.

Actual diversion of education funds from public schools to public institutions such as zoos, museums, libraries and parks could be implemented if the number of public school pupils decline substantially and as other organizations increase their usefulness as learning systems. Non-government public institutions, such as community centers and local playhouses, might receive funds if local interests desire such an arrangement. Federal and state sources of funds should permit maximum discretion at the local level.

The extent of public funding need not exceed present levels, because private sources fill out the balance of life's learning system. Movie theaters, bookstores, record shops, newsstands, magazine racks, radio and television are all learning systems that put us in touch with a variety of media.

Individual publications often become learning systems in themselves. *The Christian Science Monitor*, for instance, has reading rooms all over the world. *National Geographic Magazine* is only one arm of a learning system that produces historical and scientific programs for commercial television, films and sound filmstrips for schools, books for the general public, and that sponsors scientific expeditions and research projects.

Smithsonian Magazine's colorful pages communicate the various activities of the famous Smithsonian Institute, informative articles, and the Institute's travel tours. *Consumer Reports* conducts its own studies of consumer products, and has published a number of books and annual consumer guides.

Commercial publications, such as the *Sears & Roebuck Catalog*, contain a wealth of information about products and prices, while *Whole Earth Catalog* sales underwrite a non-profit corporation, POINT, which publishes *CoEvolution Quarterly* and supports educational innovation. *The Journal of the New Alchemists* (Woods Hole, Massachusetts) reports on their ecological technology research at several sites.

Mother Earth News reveals the details of modern homesteading and natural living, while *Prevention's* Rodale Press publishes gardening periodicals, numerous books, and operates its own organic cafeteria and food co-op. The Rodale fortune has graced its home environment with a velodrome, where bicycle enthusiasts and Olympic riders experience the rush of motorless speed; a new community theater for intimate live performances; and extensive agricultural research facilities.

The sources of learning are limitless when we stop viewing education only in terms of schools. But the learning system approach does not preclude diplomas or certificates. Those who feel they need school for their goals should go to school. Drill, lecture and other school techniques all work when the learner is committed to the effort. But we should try to recognize the importance of learning beyond school.

I have often heard people discuss Montessori school,[119] which is really a learning system, in terms of the difficulty a child will have adjusting to regular school after attending a non-structured program. We seem to think that the problem lies with the non-structured approach, never questioning the value of school.

Why do we ask whether a non-structured approach hurts performance in school? Why don't we ask whether a structured school hurts performance in real life? It is more important to practice life-long learning than formal learning. It is more important to learn on one's own than to depend on others. After graduation, who will update knowledge as the world rushes on? Who will make personal decisions when choices arise?

Schools limit individual initiative and restrict learners' choices. They do not trust people to guide themselves. Learning systems do. They give the learner only what is sought, and allow responsibility for learning to rest where it belongs—squarely on the learner's shoulders.

We must take learning systems more seriously. Public television in the United States, one of the most significant learning systems, is a national disgrace. Although the value of Sesame Street and The Electric Company is obvious, they still depend on donations from big corporations. And the best dramatic programs are produced by Britain's BBC. If only a teeny-tiny fraction of the tax money now dumped into schools went into public television production, the results would be phenomenal.[120]

But public television lost support in the past by imposing "highbrow" programming on a public that was not receptive. Ratings were low because public television failed to follow Dewey's maxim about starting where the learner is. The Children's Television Workshop did not make the same mistake and has attracted a huge audience, even among adults who find the popular children's program most entertaining.

The keys to the learning system approach are based in individual, family and community. When children see magazines and books being read in their homes, when parents read as much as they watch television, when trips to the library and museum are part of family life, when people in the community take an active interest in young people, when businesses and municipalities help find meaningful direct experiences for young people, then learning systems really work.

The learning systems I propose to build in a rural area will depend on the investment of time by interested citizens who want to experiment with community learning. Not just aimed at young counterculture types, but at conservative Pennsylvania Germans; retired people with time on their hands; professionals; factory workers; or anyone who can relate to the idea. There is no membership fee and individuals can come and go as they please. The only binding force is a sense of trust and cooperation and a feeling that we are all learners with an important common goal.

William Irwin Thompson suggests in *Quest/77* (July/August 1977) that small communities must arise that harness the wind and sun, focus on organic gardening and replacement of fossil fuel agribusiness, produce bicycles, clothing, Rototillers, or other well-crafted, durable technology, and that the entire village must be a contemplative, educational community. "At the various stages of life...the entire community would function as a college in which children and adults worked together in gardening, construction, crafts, and classes in all fields of knowledge."

Utopian dreams? Perhaps. But the unrealistic suicide trip of modern industrial society seems more foolish than Thompson's ideas: not no technology, but new technology. Not violent revolution, but purposeful evolution. Not turning back the clock, but transcending the clock. Life can be very different than it is now.

BEYOND THE SCHOOLHOUSE: Learning In A New Reality

Change is inevitable, but the nature of change has a great deal to do with our own decisions.

If we trap ourselves in our own cynicism, if we ignore the incredible curiosity of small children and its gradual destruction in the schools, if we blind ourselves to imaginative possibilities, we are truly avoiding the meaning of life. Life, it seems to me, is not endlessly acting out the rituals of the past, but thoughtfully acting on the needs of the present, with consideration and respect for the future.

Nobody knows all the answers. We must learn together, and young people whose minds have not been boxed in classrooms, may teach us as much as we teach them. Tolerance for their ideas fosters tolerance for ours. In this life, we only get what we give. And if we give love and understanding, if we assume that we all have something to learn and to teach, if we open ourselves to personal new growth—the learning system of life will draw us together in a mutually beneficial journey of new experience and knowledge.

CHAPTER **25**

Being Our Own Heroes

For almost two centuries after William Penn[121] founded his colony, Pennsylvanians grew their own food, made their own things, and built their own homes. Durham boats carried Washington across the Delaware, and Conestoga wagons carried Americans across the continent. In rural areas, small farmers were almost totally self-sufficient, growing a wide variety of crops in small quantities, which they used themselves or bartered in exchange for local crafts and services. As late as 1860, the *Potter County Journal* advertised many shoemakers, furniture makers, and blacksmiths.

The railroads and factories of the industrial age brought cheaper machine-made goods from the cities to the country, and self-sufficiency began to wane. Farmers specialized in one or two crops, sold for cash to buy manufactured consumer goods, packaged foods, machinery, fuel, and eventually fertilizers. Now Pennsylvanians get meat from Montana, cars from Detroit, oil from Kuwait, shoes from Taiwan, and artichokes from California.

But as economist E.F. Schumacher[122] points out in his book, *Small Is Beautiful: Economics As If People Mattered* (1973),[123] the existence of international industrialism rests on a false assumption: that there will always be an inexhaustible supply of cheap natural resources. One Illinois farmer correctly admitted in 1857: "We are... skinning God's heritage, taking the cream off, and leaving for parts unknown, until humanity has a heavy bill against us for wasting the vital energies of Mother Earth."

We have deluded ourselves into believing that we have solved "the problem of production," when we only have postponed it. As the soil demands bigger and bigger doses of petrochemical fertilizer to maintain crop yields against declining natural fertility, as clean water supplies dwindle, as the cost of shipping goods from hither to thither climbs steadily, as fuel grows scarcer and more expensive to produce and transport, as the environmental consequences of burning fossil fuels mount—the bill collector is knocking at our door.

The rise of industry and agribusiness was accompanied by the growth of government. Encouraged by the need to regulate the abuses of business and to provide services required by its dislocations, government assumed responsibilities for family and community. The small units yielded to big units, independence to dependence, self-sufficiency to helplessness.

Cut off from nature, modern folks make jokes about farmers, pursue their specialized tasks, and pay others to do everything else for them. Yet many lament the rising costs of life, as if they had nothing to do with the problem. It's always the politicians, television, big oil companies, bureaucracies, unions, and other external factors.

Even those who want to help improve the situation are often confused (including myself). They look to political campaigns, institutional change, and large-scale means of reform; they become frustrated with their personal inability to affect anything. But Schumacher suggests that we think small.

Being Our Own Heroes | **chapter 25**

Everywhere people ask: 'What can I actually do?' The answer is as simple as it is disconcerting: We can, each of us, work to put our inner house in order."

A Pennsylvania county commissioner, Joseph Catania,[124] warned in March, 1977, "People must return to the old traditions of helping each other, because government is rapidly approaching the point it can't afford all the services people are asking.

"Help your community go back to the old concept of caring for thy neighbors," he urged. "Government can no longer keep the people. People have had it, they are fed up with taxes. We got the message at the last budget hearing."

He said it's "up to the people, not the government, to start resolving problems. People must start caring for one another and not live under the impression the government will care for them."

We are starting to get the message. Successful society does not rest on the structure of government or big economic units. The building blocks of healthy living are individual, family, and community. They are also the building blocks of healthy learning, and are the alternative to the expensive structure of schools.

I have known people who taught themselves cabinetmaking, history, gardening, macramé, welding, foreign languages, swimming, carpentry, beekeeping, plumbing, astronomy, guitar, and scores of other skills and areas of knowledge, without professional teachers or schools. They had enough self-confidence to seek resources or skilled individuals on their own, steered by their curiosity and determination.[125]

And I have seen people learn enough about "homemade" and "homegrown" to drastically reduce their dependence on the money system. Their efforts have made me wonder if maybe I could learn to do some of those things, making myself and my family less vulnerable to the whims of modern civilization. For until now, I have been a specialist, working in a modern job and paying for almost all my basic needs.

The small farmer overspecialized and was destroyed when the market for a single crop fell, much like the overspecialized technician or degree holder, whose slice of the job market fails. Without learning how to take care of our own basic needs, we are at the mercy of callous economic forces. Without a diversity of enterprise, whole communities are destroyed with the closing of a single industrial plant.

We must learn to do more for ourselves as individuals, as families, as communities. We must build a better society from the bottom up, on a strong foundation of small social units with diverse functions and cooperative methods.

We must begin to guide ourselves, to be our own heroes. Each community has a unique set of circumstances and resources that can only be developed on a local basis. Jimmy Carter and the state governor, Barbara Walters and Johnny Carson, Stevie Wonder and Gloria Steinem, Henry Kissinger and Ralph Nader are all too remote to help us. John F. Kennedy's words must be rephrased: "Ask not what your country can do for you, ask what you can do for yourself, your family, and your community."

Susan and I, Josh and Benji, came back from California to our community. We came back to our family and friends. There are no greener pastures, as best as I can see, just dark clouds gathering everywhere. Drought, smog, pollution, highways and buildings decaying faster than we can repair them, old dams bursting as water runs off new parking lots and housing developments, floodplains rising, cancer rampant in industrial areas, costs sky high, insecure Social Security, old people abandoned in cities, joblessness, dislocation, alienation, macabre killings, urban terror.

My family has traveled through our nation seeking a lost dream. And we could sense emptiness in many people.

Celebrating the Bicentennial by my personal revolution, I have the feeling that our nation has lost something along the way. The spirit of independence, Jefferson's land of small farmers, individuality, integrity, personal touch, peace of mind. Not even the Founding Fathers can help us now. We are strictly on our own.

BEYOND THE SCHOOLHOUSE: Learning In A New Reality

CHAPTER 26

All the Kind People

I am building the first component of a learning system in the community where I lived and worked for eight years. When I first came to the community in 1968, it was still nestled in a "happy valley" which had changed to the temper of our troubled times before I left in 1976. A rural area becoming suburban: housing developments, sewer projects, new roads, parking lots, shopping centers, neon signs, and the signs of "progress." A community in flux.

There are many kind people in the community. The couple across the street who used to share their chestnuts with us; the neighbors with the collie, who played with our kids; the East German family with whom we shared good times and bad; local political acquaintances; friends; the librarians who supported me through thick and thin; administrators and teachers who encouraged me; secretaries and custodians who told me "what was happening," or loaned me keys to work at night on a deadline project; the superintendent and school board members who watched me grow up and my co-workers who watched me grow unhappy.

Among the kind people in the community who are still young enough to remember what school was like and to imagine how it could be different. They are the most important people in the community for my learning system model. Their children will attend public schools unless they do something about it. Like the two young men on the church council that is sharing its facilities, they are in a position to lend a helping hand or a kind word.

The Class of 1970, which whom I was the closest, graduated high school during the Vietnam War and campus unrest. They dedicated their yearbook to me and another teacher, and then scattered through the world. I have seen some of them from time to time, and a few have become personal friends. I sense in them the same frustration with the modern world and its lack of enthusiasm for our generation's dreams.

But our generation's dreams are only modifications of our parents' dreams, and the dreams of our ancestors. Each generation responds to a changing world with a new image of the future. There are kind people of all ages, who have grown with life's challenges and are open to new ideas.

Like my parents, who have generously housed us while we assemble our affairs. Like Susan's mother and her father, whose recent death moved his community to express its appreciation of his kindness. And all the kind people who have helped us along our way. Friends. Relatives. Even strangers who have shown the unexpected kindness that brightens the grayness of a bad day.

And all the writers whose ideas merged in my mind. And all the music people who have fed my head with the sounds of their kindest thoughts. And all those fools who have struggled in pursuit of their ideals.

If only all the kind people in the world could get together and establish a new reality based on kindness…a new reality that can heal our wounds and turn us toward healthier purposes. A new reality that trusts in diversity and cooperation. A new reality that trusts in dreams.

CHAPTER **27**

Dreaming of a New Reality

Energy bolts from pursuing Imperial fighters burst on his Y-Wing shields as Star Wars' hero zeroed in for the long shot. Trying to fire a torpedo into an emergency exhaust port of the moon-size battle station was like shooting a thread through a needle's eye.

"Use the Force, Luke. Let go."

Hearing this voice of his martyred mentor, Ben Kenobi, echoing in his head, Luke pushed aside his computerized targeting screen and fired when his feelings commanded.

"Remember, the Force will be with you, always," said the voice.

The technological monster burst into gaseous flame, ending the evil reign of the Galactic Empire. The universe was at peace and a new age of goodness prevailed.

If Alexei[126] and Cory Panshin[127] are correct about science fiction being "the ideal reflection of the world around us," then *Star Wars*[128] is reflecting an idealized version of the changes that are occurring around us. In their *SF in Dimension: A Book of Explorations*,[129] they argue that science fiction might more appropriately be called speculative fantasy, which frees it from its technological origins and "allows the possibility of stepping outside the limitations of the present moment and considering the alternatives."[130]

I have known the Panshins for several years, and have watched them struggle and spin their dreams of a new conception of SF to an audience that was not quite prepared for their message. Now as their fortunes seem to rise, I understand more fully the power of personal vision, and I am spinning some dreams of my own. Their words and deeds have helped guide the way:

The purpose of fantasy is consciousness expansion. The existence of unconsciousness, and the existence of unknown things in the world around us, force us to expand the borders of the known.

In *Star Wars* (1976), the unconscious mind is symbolized by "the Force." George Lucas,[131] the author of the book and producer of the film, explains the Force through the character of Ben Kenobi, speaking to young Luke.

"Scientists theorized it is an energy field generated by living things. Early man suspected its existence, yet remained in ignorance of its potential for millennia...The Force surrounds each and every one of us."

I saw *Star Wars* when this book was well underway, and my projected outline was fairly complete. I was stunned to find that the motion picture had anticipated much of what I was writing about. The whole notion of following feelings, not just reason: the idea of a new religious era, an ecumenical rebirth of the spiritual; Julian Jayne's voices of the gods; the characteristics of the right hemisphere. It was all there in *Star Wars*.

Instructing Luke on the use of the Force in life. Kenobi says, "You must try to divorce your actions from conscious control. Try not to focus on anything concrete...You have to enter a state in which you act on what you sense, not on what you think beforehand."

Jules Verne[132] predicted submarines and moon travel before the turn of the century. George Lucas predicts a change in human behavior and spiritual feeling. Those who are skeptical should consider the magnitude of the response to *Star Wars* and the futility of Jules Verne doubters. Friendly, trusting Luke and "liberated" Princess Leia became new American heroes.

Millions of Americans, particularly the young, are being bound together by a new myth. And *Star Wars* is likely to command a huge international audience, as well. Something about the film fills a need, closes a gap, provides an image of the universe that most find appealing.

And that's what dreaming is all about. Without dreams, we stumble around in the darkness, seeing nothing.

I remember reading a little book by Henry W. Simon, *What Is A Teacher?* (1938, 1964), when I first entered the profession. He suggested that I accept school as a hard fact.

> *When, however, society becomes more complex, when it requires of its young such complicated skills as reading and writing or a more advanced method of warfare—skills that not every adult in the community himself possesses—it is necessary to engage a schoolmaster and to set up the institution of the school…and you cannot alter a fact by wishing it were different.*

But I became unhappy with the school's obsessive emphasis on reading and writing and cared less about a more advanced method of warfare and society's complexity. As I confronted the fact of school in my job, I began to wish it were different. It wasn't foolish or irrelevant: that is the first step one must take to alter a fact.

I tried to plant a magic bean in the schoolyard, and watched it grow toward the sky. But when I climbed my dreamstalk, I found that someone kept chopping at its stem, someone else had already run off with the goose that laid the golden eggs, and mostly skeptics inhabited the castle in the clouds.

Henry David Thoreau[133] said: "If you have built castles in the air, your work need not be lost; that is where they should be. Now put the foundations under them." But I couldn't do it—not in the school. Not surrounded by so many people who no longer trust in dreams, who kill dreams in their students, their colleagues and themselves, who can only imagine what is already there.

Somehow, many have come to believe that dreaming is a silly notion that isn't of any use in this cold, cruel, practical world. Perhaps they have suffered the numbing frustration of trying to be human in a dehumanized institutional setting. But dreaming is essential to being human, and acting upon dreams is essential to being happy. Although we may not attain our dreams in our lifetime, like Moses who never entered the Promised Land, we can help humanity along on its way.

When we stop dreaming, we die. Oh, we may walk around for a while, taking up space. But life without dreams is death, and America has become the land of the living dead, endlessly following well-worn paths. Too many have allowed their imaginations to be crushed by the doubts of zombies, and now find themselves sharing the same fate.

I visited a young man in Philadelphia who was about to graduate college this spring. He said that he wanted to be a writer, but everyone around him discouraged his dream. They said it wasn't practical, that he should pursue a more realistic career. I listened to him with deep empathy. All I could say was that I understood his situation well and that if I were him, knowing what I know now, I would opt for my dream and ignore the dream killers.

Da Vinci, Mozart, Poe, Edison were all dreamers who saw images in their minds and pursued them. Even Alfred Korzybski,[134] who invented modern semantics—the study of word meanings—claimed he thought in pictures, not words. Right hemisphere dreaming is fundamental to creative change, made practical by left hemisphere analysis. Einstein said that imagination is more important than knowledge. And Friedrich August Kekule[135] awoke from a dream of six snakes arranged in a hexagon, and predicted the molecular structure of benzene. He told the incredulous scientists of the 19th century, "Let us learn to dream, gentleman, and then, no doubt, we will discover the truth."

In my own dreams, I see communities growing stronger, becoming more independent, providing for their own welfare, using land and water more carefully, recycling their own wastes, creating local food sources and productive enterprises without the uncertainty of large-scale economics, implementing innovations in energy use, transportation, health services, and "cottage industry" approaches to the care of the very young, the very old, and the very handicapped on a neighborhood, people-size basis.

I dream of a new reality in which we are learners from birth to death, enjoying the game but not keeping score, emphasizing cooperation over competition, quality over success, satisfaction over money. An idealistic dream but not utopian.

Dreamers must ultimately accept imperfection. However, in today's modern world we glorify imperfection, restricting ourselves to the limitations of industrial society and trading our dreams for a very impractical reality.

BEYOND THE SCHOOLHOUSE: Learning In A New Reality

CHAPTER 28

A Practical Matter

Survival. While scheming and dreaming the Community Service Foundation[136] into existence, we have struggled to survive economically. Spending all the money from the sale of our house, our savings, borrowing more money, living with parents, taking adolescent foster children into our home, we have managed to survive without earning any income from our efforts to establish an alternative to schooling.

Until now. We have finally emerged from the tunnel. Two years after leaving my job in the public schools, the Community Service Foundation has attained a contract to operate an alternative program for young people, under the auspices of the juvenile probation system.

Idealistic dreams are becoming real as we begin to demonstrate a new concept of learning, with youth that society has labeled "delinquent." Which brings us to another practical matter: Effectiveness.

Unless my ideas prove effective with youth who are alienated from conventional schooling, the Foundation's contract will lapse and I will be left holding my dreams. Reality can be a cruel master. Nonetheless, I am confident that the Community Service Foundation will fulfill its task.

BEYOND THE SCHOOLHOUSE: Learning In A New Reality

CHAPTER 29

Future Without Limits

Magic.

We are reaching beyond the known into the unknown, for magic. Mysterious, until the magic becomes known. Then we call it knowledge.

Since the dawn of humankind, we have pursued the mysterious. My favorite physicist, Albert Einstein, said, "The most beautiful things we can experience is the mysterious. It is the source of all true art and science."

The mystery of human intelligence has given way to a great deal of new knowledge in recent years. Knowledge that has implications for our lives now, if we put it to use. If we rely on the obsolete information from our school days, we are sure to ignore the revolutionary change occurring in front of our eyes: the children of television.

Despite much shoddy programming, the integrative television medium has balanced the relationship between the dominant left brain and the deprived right brain. We must now learn to use our two brains to look at the universe on two levels, simultaneously: The level of dreams, and the level of reality.

There are no guarantees in our search for new knowledge. We may fall on our collective face and break our beak. Or fly like an eagle.

"But we must not judge the society of the future by considering whether or not we should like to live in it," said Bertrand Russell.[137] "The question is whether those who have grown up in it will be happier than those who have grown up in our society or those of the past."

If we cannot imagine learning without schools, we place limits on the future. We must face the fact that Egyptians do not build pyramids anymore. Our most sacred institutions will someday cease to exist, because the conditions they were born to serve no longer exist. Why do we think that public schools will last forever?

In a rapidly evolving society that invents and abandons like a fashion model changes clothes, why are we invested in thinking the public schools will even last our lifetime?

CHAPTER **30**

A New Day

And as you cross the wilderness
Spinning in your emptiness
You feel you have to pray
Looking for a sign
That the universal mind
Has written you into the passion play
Skating away, skating away
Skating away, on the thin ice of a new day

Crossing the Colorado River into California, we greeted the dawning sun with Jethro Tull's song ringing in our ears. The Mojave Desert stretched away from us in all directions, as we opened the curtains in our window van.

Our destination, Laguna Beach, was a few hours away, and we shared a strong sense of anticipation as we neared the Pacific shore.

A new day.

Looking at our journey from the perspective of two years later, I know that some of our dreams would be realized. But at the time,

I was scared and unsure. I suppose that I still am, but now I pay less attention to my fears and more attention to what seems to be unfolding around us:

A new day.

There is no specific moment when the new day begins. It begins when you perceive its beginning. Each individual recognizes a new day at his or her own moment, and in his or her own way.

As the tumult of the old day stills itself, darkness sets in. Awaiting the new day, we live in darkness. That seems to be the global mood. Darkness.

But we can pass the time of darkness by turning to our own needs. By learning how to cooperate in our own communities. And by trusting in the onset of a new day.

Epilogue

"And by trusting in the onset of a new day."

That's how I originally ended this book in 1977. But I'm no longer merely dreaming of a new reality. Rather, I and many others are building it. My website, *buildinganewreality.com*, highlights both longstanding efforts and new possibilities.

A chapter in my book shares the vision that Kenneth Silber described in his 1972 article, "The Learning System," which became integral to the way I imagine the future. Silber described the game of guessing "What's Wrong with America's Public Schools?" Despite efforts at reform, he asked, "Why have all these reforms had no real effect? The answer is, I believe, twofold: the magnitude and complexity of the school system, and failure to look at basic assumptions."

His words still ring true. Schools have become more bureaucratic, and educational reformers still "never ask the real questions about learning and about what kinds of institutions best facilitate it."

In January, 2018, shortly after I made the decision to finally publish my 40-year-old book, a friend brought to my attention an article[138] by Valerie Strauss in *The Washington Post* about the

Philadelphia schools. It included an open letter from a distinguished educational researcher, David Berliner. He offered advice to the school district's new leadership, who would soon restore local control of the schools to the city of Philadelphia, after more than 17 years of state control.

Berliner affirmed a lot of what I believe about the foolishness of blaming teachers for poor educational outcomes and the significance of socioeconomic factors that influence test scores as much as, or more than, anything else. But he never looks beyond the schoolhouse. The letter's author is a traditional expert, who still thinks and writes only in terms of school-based learning.

Colleagues of mine and I have done a great deal of training and consulting in the Philadelphia schools, where I have seen such exciting potential in kids. But I have also seen how utterly bored and resentful many are with what's being forced upon them. A familiar adage warns that you can lead a horse to water, but you can't make it drink.

We keep trying to fix the schools, forcing children to attend them, when we should be thinking beyond the schoolhouse. As Marshall McLuhan,[139] the Canadian media scholar, pointed out in the 1970's, with the advent of television, the information level outside the schools became higher than inside. The information explosion fostered by the Internet has exponentially magnified that dilemma. The challenge facing schools is much like that described in the old World War One song: "How Ya Gonna Keep 'em Down on the Farm After They've Seen Paree [Paris]?"

As a young Pennsylvania educator, in 1972 I was inspired by the newly appointed state Secretary of Education, John C. Pittenger,[140] who advocated for more "learning by doing," in lieu of formal schooling. He recognized that many students graduated from high school without actually knowing how to function in the real world. But I and others who wanted to act on his suggestions felt abandoned when he left Pennsylvania to teach at Harvard in 1976.

Epilogue

I decided to leave the public schools as well, establishing a number of alternative schools, group homes and counseling programs for delinquent and at-risk youth in Pennsylvania,[141] where I could try out my unconventional ideas. I eventually founded a freestanding, accredited, master's-degree-granting graduate school[142] to teach "restorative practices," an emerging social science that has demonstrated the efficacy of our strategies to help challenging young people and struggling schools.

Instead of doing things to and for young people, we show professionals how to engage and do things with them. Restorative practices give young people more voice and more choice, but also more responsibility. Because restorative practices are effective, interest has grown dramatically. The International Institute for Restorative Practices (IIRP) now provides professional development in restorative practices throughout the U.S. and around the world—currently training more than 25,000 teachers and other youth-serving professionals each year.

Beyond the schoolhouse, there are now precedents for learning by doing and self-directed learning, in lieu of formal schooling, that could accomplish two things:

1. Alternatives to school would liberate classrooms from those who don't want to be there, leaving them filled only with kids who choose to be there: a teacher's dream come true.

2. For less money than the cost of public schools, alternatives to school would get kids who don't want to be in school out into the real world.

Young people could be involved in non-school activities that they choose, that help them learn critical social and employment skills that schools don't teach, and possibly earn some modest income. I'm only half joking when I suggest that we should bring back child labor. There are so many creative possibilities that have yet to be tried.

We confuse learning with schooling. Learning continues to be measured by the number of years in school and the number of diplomas collected. Informal learning, acquired through direct experience, or self-directed learning, driven by personal interest, are still regarded as inferior to school learning. Yet, there is a growing resistance to school and the hallmark measure of school progress: standardized testing. In 2016, a half-million schoolchildren opted out of standardized testing. [143]

One of the most dramatic developments since I wrote my book in 1977 is the growth of the homeschooling movement. In 2016, the parents of 2.3 million American children of school age—more than three percent—refused to send their children to school at all, and home-schooled them instead.[144]

Parents who homeschool may supervise their children's education themselves, and may employ a variety of resources such as museums, libraries, zoos, sports clubs and other youth-serving organizations. Still other homeschoolers may turn to self-directed learning programs that are not schools, but alternatives to school.

An Alternative to School

When I first read Ivan Illich's book, *Deschooling Society*,[145] and Silber's "Learning Systems" article,[146] I tried to imagine what an alternative to school would look like. While my own alternative schools were a step in the right direction, others have moved much farther down the road.

Ken Danford, a former middle school teacher, co-founded North Star Self-Directed Learning for Teens[147] in 1996 in western Massachusetts, out of his concern for his students who hated school and who were struggling academically and emotionally.

Willow—now in her thirties—was good student, but was miserable. Her dream was to become a children's librarian, but she felt

Epilogue

socially alienated in her public school. Instead, she spent four years at the newly created North Star program, went to college, and is now a children's librarian.

Willow has since told Danford: "School was really bad for me. Sometimes I wonder if I would have survived four years of high school. I think maybe you saved my life."

North Star is now the model for a network called Liberated Learners,[148] which assists new self-directed learning programs in getting started. Northstar Self Directed Learning for Teens demonstrates one of the most critical changes needed to create a new reality: ending the monopoly that schools have on the resources our society devotes to learning.

Self-directed learning and learning by doing are rarely employed in school settings. Even if some schools attempt to imitate real life, the carrot and the stick of grades change the nature of the experience to one of anxiety for everyone: students, parents and teachers. School often turns experiences that could be fun into fearful ones, even for the best students.

Many people believe that evaluation in school prepares you for the workplace, but that's not true. There are few work settings that evaluate so many small component tasks in such an intrusive way.

In work settings, you are evaluated for your overall job performance, at a job you choose and are paid to do. But under the compulsory school monopoly, no one gets to choose whether they go to school and no one gets paid. School grading systems reward those who like school, and shames those who don't.

The standardized testing system dictates a narrow perception of what is worth learning—things we can readily test, but which may not actually meet students' needs or wants, or even be relevant as life skills.

The North Star Self-Directed Learning program, on the other hand, restores choice and makes learning enjoyable. By eliminating mandates, tests and grades, North Star allows young people to take responsibility for their own learning—making choices and motivating themselves—the way people learn naturally, in real life.

Adults at North Star assist young people as facilitators, not dictators, whose role is to "make possible" rather than "make sure." They help young people choose their activities, including those that North Star itself offers—from learning a musical instrument to a variety of classes taught without tests or grades.

My son Josh, who taught and advised students at North Star, invited my wife, Susan, and I to a fundraising event. There we heard one of North Star's former learners speak about how, despite hating high school, he started to attend community college classes because he chose to do so. Without ever having graduated high school, he went on to graduate from college, as do many North Star kids, because he chose to do so.

There are currently a dozen learning programs in the Liberated Learners network, based on the North Star model, and more on the way. While North Star relies on tuition and charitable donations, the challenge ultimately will be to bring this approach to scale, so that it can accommodate large numbers of young people in areas where there are few parents who can afford tuition.

The political challenge of diverting public money from schools to the alternatives will be formidable. But I still trust in the onset of a new day, when society will finally acknowledge the truth of the North Star slogan: "Learning is natural. School is optional."[149]

Notes

1. Skating Away

1 - "How To Grow A School," https://www.amazon.com/How-Grow-School-Starting-Sustaining/dp/0945700067

2 - Dewey quote, http://www.tandfonline.com/doi/abs/10.1080/00131728609335764

3 - "Deschooling Society," https://en.wikipedia.org/wiki/Deschooling_Society

4 - George Gallup quote, http://journals.sagepub.com/doi/pdf/10.1177/019263657505939101

5 - "I Ching" reference, https://books.google.com/books?id=FynLUDw20rsC&pg=RA1-PA76#v=onepage&q&f=false

6 - George Santayana quote, https://en.wikiquote.org/wiki/George_Santayana

7 - …without even learning reading, writing and arithmetic, https://www.theatlantic.com/education/archive/2018/04/-american-students-reading/557915/

2. Compulsory Education

8 - "How To Survive In Your Native Land," https://www.nytimes.com/1971/04/11/archives/how-to-survive-in-your-native-land-by-james-herndon-192-pp-new-york.html

3. A Century of Coercion

9 - Thomas Jefferson Memorial, https://en.wikipedia.org/wiki/Jefferson_Memorial

BEYOND THE SCHOOLHOUSE: Learning In A New Reality

10 - Massachusetts made public education mandatory, http://education.findlaw.com/education-options/compulsory-education-laws-background.html

11 - Jefferson reference, https://millercenter.org/president/jefferson/life-before-the-presidency

12 - consolidation movement, https://sites.hks.harvard.edu/pepg/PDF/Papers/PEPG05-04%20Berry%20West.pdf

13 - National Institute of Education study, https://files.eric.ed.gov/fulltext/ED135507.pdf

4. Aims and Means

14 - ...the aim must be the training of independently acting and thinking individuals, https://www.nytimes.com/1974/04/16/archives/the-motorcycles-of-your-mind-books-of-the-times.html

15 - "Zen and the Art of Motorcycle Maintenance" reference, http://www.nytimes.com/1974/04/16/archives/the-motorcycles-of-your-mind-books-of-the-times.html

16 - ...corporal punishment serves important educational interests, http://blogs.edweek.org/edweek/school_law/2008/06/the_supreme_court_and_corporal.html

17 - The 1977 Supreme Court decision allowing corporal punishment still is the law of the land, although most states have banned it from their schools. Nineteen states still allow schools to administer corporal punishment. https://www.washingtonpost.com/news/answer-sheet/wp/2014/09/18/19-states-still-allow-corporal-punishment-in-school

5. Measuring the Marigolds

18 - Hans Christian Anderson, https://en.wikipedia.org/wiki/Hans_Christian_Andersen_(film)

19 - Kuder Preference Test, https://www.kuder.com/about/history-legacy

Notes

6. Lines That Divide

20 - …resolve their own speech defects, https://www.speechbuddy.com/blog/speech-therapist/outgrow-speech-impediment

7. The Cloistered Classroom

21 - John C. Pittenger, https://en.wikipedia.org/wiki/John_Pittenger

22 - "The Medium is the Message," https://en.wikipedia.org/wiki/The_medium_is_the_message

23 - Parkway Program, https://eric.ed.gov/?id=ED075534

8. Too Many Blacksmiths

24 - study, http://psycnet.apa.org/record/1965-06012-001

25 - Taylor confirmed what previous studies had already shown, http://www.ibric.net/WEBSTUFF/IBRICHistoryD.pdf

9. Writing on the Wall

26 - …comprehensive study of school violence, http://webapp1.dlib.indiana.edu/findingaids/view?doc.view=entire_text&docId=VAD0438

10. Freedom of Education

27 - William Penn's colony, http://www.upenn.edu/pennpress/book/1806.html

28 - James Herndon, https://en.wikipedia.org/wiki/James_Herndon_(writer)

29 - William Douglas, https://en.wikipedia.org/wiki/William_O._Douglas

Part Two

30 - Krishnamurti, 1970, http://www.jkrishnamurti.org/krishnamurti-teachings/print.php?tid=17&chid=592

11. Something Else

31 - "Black Elk Speaks," https://en.wikipedia.org/wiki/Black_Elk_Speaks

BEYOND THE SCHOOLHOUSE: Learning In A New Reality

12. Split Brain

32 - Roger Sperry and Ronald Myers cut the connection between the two halves of a cat's cerebrum, https://www.jstor.org/stable/20298126

33 - Sperry and Michael Gazzaniga studied humans whose brains had been split, https://www.psychologytoday.com/blog/the-superhuman-mind/201211/split-brains

34 - Pierre Paul Broca and Carl Warnicke, http://www.psychologyconcepts.com/brocas-and-wernickes-areas

35 - Scientific American article, https://www.scientificamerican.com/magazine/sa/1967/08-01

36 - article, https://www.cia.gov/library/readingroom/docs/CIA-RDP96-00787R000200080040-0.pdf

37 - Solomon Katz's study, https://books.google.com/books?id=0J7TaTTxKikC&pg=PA8

38 - "The Dragons of Eden," https://en.wikipedia.org/wiki/The_Dragons_of_Eden

39 - article, http://calteches.library.caltech.edu/3008/1/lab.pdf

40 - Research reported in 2013 challenged the notion in popular culture that the terms "left-brained" and "right-brained" refer to personality types, based on the assumption that people who use the right side of their brains more are more creative, thoughtful and subjective, while those who tap the left side more are more logical, detail-oriented and analytical. http://www.apa.org/monitor/2013/11/right-brained.aspx

Research reported in 2017 challenged Sperry's and Gazzaniga's claim that cutting the corpus callosum that connects the left and right brain results in a separate consciousness in each. https://www.sciencedaily.com/releases/2017/01/170125093823.htm

However, neither of these findings contradict my 1977 concern that schools favor left-brain learning over right-brain learning.

Notes

13. A Change Of Mind

41 - Julian Jaynes' book, https://en.wikipedia.org/wiki/Julian_Jaynes

42 - Ernest R. Hilgard, https://en.wikipedia.org/wiki/Ernest_Hilgard

43 - Christopher Lehmann-Haupt, https://en.wikipedia.org/wiki/Christopher_Lehmann-Haupt

44 - Sadly, the use of fear, police and military control in the decades since Jayne's book was published continues to confirm his assertion.

14. Bits and Pieces

45 - Madeleine Hunter, https://en.wikipedia.org/wiki/Madeline_Cheek_Hunter

46 - The 1977 school terminology which designated subjects as "minor" or "major" is no longer in use.

47 - …debating the merits of oral truth versus written truth, http://www.gradesaver.com/phaedrus/study-guide/summary-discussion-of-writing-274b-277a

48 - Robert Ornstein, https://en.wikipedia.org/wiki/Robert_E._Ornstein

49 - "The Psychology of Consciousness," https://www.goodreads.com/book/show/746199.The_Psychology_of_Consciousness

50 - Idries Shah, https://en.wikipedia.org/wiki/Idries_Shah

51 - In 1977, the electronic stream of voice, music and images was limited to cinema and television. Today's Internet, like a torrential rainstorm, has turned the electronic stream into a raging digital river of text, voice, music, images and motion visuals. Discriminating quality and truth without the left-brained censors and media middlemen is like trying to take a sip from that river. Schools struggle to compete for their students' attention, now that information is on the loose. We must—and I trust we will—learn to navigate the currents beyond the schoolhouse.

BEYOND THE SCHOOLHOUSE: Learning In A New Reality

15. Electric Media

52 - ...a peace treaty had been signed two weeks earlier, https://en.wikipedia.org/wiki/Battle_of_New_Orleans

53 - Pony Express, https://en.wikipedia.org/wiki/Pony_Express

54 - Michael Faraday, https://en.wikipedia.org/wiki/Michael_Faraday

55 - Samuel Morse, https://en.wikipedia.org/wiki/Samuel_Morse

56 - Alexander Graham Bell, https://en.wikipedia.org/wiki/Alexander_Graham_Bell

57 - Thomas Alva Edison, https://en.wikipedia.org/wiki/Thomas_Edison

58 - Guglielmo Marconi, https://en.wikipedia.org/wiki/Guglielmo_Marconi

59 - Ellen Torgerson, https://www.upi.com/Archives/1983/04/21/Ellen-Torgerson-Shaw-a-writer-for-TV-Guide-and/4477419749200/

16. Cosmic Consciousness

60 - Richard Maurice Bucke, https://en.wikipedia.org/wiki/Richard_Maurice_Bucke

61 - Special Theory of Relativity, https://en.wikipedia.org/wiki/Special_relativity

62 - John Neihardt, https://en.wikipedia.org/wiki/John_Neihardt

63 - Black Elk, https://en.wikipedia.org/wiki/Black_Elk

64 - Charles Reich, https://en.wikipedia.org/wiki/Charles_A._Reich

65 - "The Greening of America," https://en.wikipedia.org/wiki/The_Greening_of_America

66 - "Galton's Walk," http://www.worldcat.org/title/galtons-walk-methods-for-the-analysis-of-thinking-intelligence-and-creativity/oclc/90273

67 - "Dragons of Eden," https://en.wikipedia.org/wiki/The_Dragons_of_Eden

Notes

68 - "Brain Changes in Response to Experience," https://www.scientificamerican.com/magazine/sa/1972/02-01/

69 - William Greenbough, https://news.illinois.edu/view/6367/204677

70 - Indeed, the further evidence was remarkable. William Greenbough—an early explorer of brain plasticity, whose article I cited in 1977—died in 2014. Based on the research at the time, I mistakenly understood that only children's brains could change with environmental enrichment.

However, as one of his successors explained, "He led the way in illuminating experience-related plasticity in the mammalian brain, overcoming early views that sensory and motor systems of the brain were largely fixed very early in life, showing instead that the development of new synapses occurred in response to environmental enrichment and learning." We now know that our brains can evolve throughout our lives. Digital media and other experiences are potential catalysts for a new consciousness. https://news.illinois.edu/view/6367/204677

17. Age of Genius

71 - John Debes, https://en.wikipedia.org/wiki/Visual_literacy

72 - Robert Thorndike, https://en.wikipedia.org/wiki/Robert_L._Thorndike

73 - Intelligence Quotient, https://en.wikipedia.org/wiki/Intelligence_quotient

74 - My concern about schools inhibiting growth in intelligence has been offset by the universal advent of digital media influence on our daily lives. The increasing prevalence of motion-visual communication seems the most likely cause of significant gains in IQ in the general population in countries around the world—called the Flynn effect—and the related need to keep adjusting IQ scoring, which has been done many times, from the 1930's to the present. https://en.wikipedia.org/wiki/Flynn_effect

"Attempted explanations have included improved nutrition, a trend toward smaller families, better education, greater environmental complexity, and heterosis (the occurrence of offspring with more pronounced phenotypical traits from mixing the genes of its parents). Another proposition is the gradual spread of test-taking skills. The Flynn effect has been too rapid for genetic selection to be the cause."

But no one, to my knowledge, has done research that examines the possibility suggested by Marshall McCluhan, the late Canadian media scholar: that "the medium is the message." Because research in brain plasticity has confirmed how environmental factors literally alter our brains throughout our lives, worldwide access to motion visuals, accelerated by the omnipresence of digital communication, may well be the primary cause of our species' remarkable increases in IQ scores.

75 - study, https://archive.org/stream/ERIC_ED108659/ERIC_ED108659_djvu.txt

76 - "My Life on the Plains," https://www.amazon.com/My-Life-Plains-Personal-Experiences/dp/1429021047

77 - NAEP compared test profiles of youngsters at 9, 13, and 17 years old, https://books.google.com/books?id=t39GBQAAQBAJ&pg=PA69&lpg=PA69&dq=NAEP+1977#v=onepage&q=NAEP%201977&f=false

78 - William James, https://en.wikipedia.org/wiki/William_James

79 - "Divergent," a 2011 book and 2014 film, is a dystopian science fiction story in which those labeled "Divergent" are considered threats to the existing social order, because they think independently and the government cannot control them. https://en.wikipedia.org/wiki/Divergent_(film)

80 - convergent thinking, https://en.wikipedia.org/wiki/Convergent_thinking

81 - article, https://eric.ed.gov/?q=Brain+AND+waves+AND+children&pg=4&id=EJ159535

82 - study, http://www.urigeller.com/effects-chronological-age-gesp-ability

83 - When I went back to this remarkable ESP experiment that I cited in 1977, I had trouble finding evidence of replication since then—a red flag that raised my concerns about the validity of the original experiment. I contacted the researcher, Ernesto Spinelli, who has gone on from his doctoral research in ESP to an impressive career as an academic and psychotherapist

in the United Kingdom. He responded promptly and generously, acknowledging the importance of the issue I raised. (January 10, 2018 email to me)

I will first share some of the details from an earlier description of his experiment, to illustrate how meticulous and creative he was in carrying out his study, which was part of his Ph.D. thesis. In the first round he had 1,000 subjects, aged between 3 and 70 years (which I misreported in my 1977 writing), guess images from cards with different pictures. With children between 3 and 10, he told them the experiment was a "guessing game" and used puppets to provide the instructions, removing much of the tension created in children when adult strangers tell them what to do.

The puppets made it easier and more interesting for children to learn the instructions. The children were also given "thinking caps" (cone-shaped cardboard hats covered with tin foil and wire and padded inside around the ear area) which they wore throughout the experiment. The thinking caps reinforced the experimenter's claim that the children were "playing a game" and also limited distracting outside noise. He ran several rounds with additional subjects, which replicated the first round.

In his email, he shared with me what he knew about various replication attempts, but it seems that few researchers were as thoughtful and thorough, in terms of numbers of subjects and the care he took to make children comfortable. Some also made questionable changes to the protocols.

One researcher, Susan Shargal from City University of New York, replicated his research for her 1980 Ph.D. dissertation: "ESP in Children: Its Relationship to Age and Personality," and got very similar results to Spinelli. Sadly, I could not communicate with her because she died in 2000.

He also reported that a final test was carried out in 1985 for "Arthur C. Clarke's World of Strange Powers," a popular British television series. He wrote: "I appeared on it together with a colleague and some children that the programme researchers had collected together, and a version of the studies was set up and filmed. Once again, the results were in line with my previous research findings, though, obviously, this was for television and only a small number of trials were carried out."

Finally, Spinelli sent me Chapter 9, entitled "The Great Beyond," from his 2001 book, "The Mirror and Hammer: Challenges to Therapeutic Orthodoxy" (2001) in which—with the integrity of a good scientist—he explains, "While these studies succeeded in convincing me, and a great many other researchers, that paranormal phenomena can be elicited even within the rigid and unusual conditions of a structured experiment, they have not yet been sufficiently validated by other independent studies and, as such, cannot be said to provide conclusive scientific evidence—a common recurrence in just about every attempt to study paranormal phenomena under experimental conditions!"

Nonetheless, I am now sufficiently convinced that the study I reported in 1977 was not bogus and is worthy of serious consideration.

18. Seeing the Forest

84 - massive blackout, https://en.wikipedia.org/wiki/New_York_City_blackout_of_1977

19. Children as People

85 - John Holt, https://en.wikipedia.org/wiki/John_Holt_(educator)

86 - Silvano Arieti, https://en.wikipedia.org/wiki/Silvano_Arieti

87 - "Creativity: The Magic Synthesis," https://www.goodreads.com/book/show/966116.Creativity

88 - E. Paul Torrance, https://en.wikipedia.org/wiki/Ellis_Paul_Torrance

89 - "Education and the Creative Potential," https://muse.jhu.edu/book/31773

20. Life as Learning

90 - 1964 World's Fair, https://en.wikipedia.org/wiki/1964_New_York_World's_Fair

91 - "The World of Tomorrow," https://en.wikipedia.org/wiki/1939_New_York_World%27s_Fair

92 - Alfred North Whitehead, https://en.wikipedia.org/wiki/Alfred_North_Whitehead

Notes

93 - Coney Island parachute jump, https://en.wikipedia.org/wiki/Parachute_Jump

94 - "The Last Whole Earth Catalog," https://en.wikipedia.org/wiki/Whole_Earth_Catalog

95 - Community Service Foundation, csfbuxmont.org

96 - As of 2018, the Community Service Foundation has been around for more than forty years. With its academic partner, Buxmont Academy, we deal with the most challenging youth from schools and courts. Each youth must decide whether they want to be with us before they can enroll, regardless of the reason that they are referred to us. Our strategies rely on giving young people "more voice, more choice and more responsibility."

Their learning is less about academics—which usually improves—and more about behavior. A three-phase study—from 1999 to 2006—with almost 4,000 youth, found that not only did participants learn new behaviors, but the research showed more than a fifty percent reduction in criminal offending. https://www.iirp.edu/news/community-service-foundation-and-buxmont-academy-csf-buxmont-analysis-of-students-discharged-during-three-school-years-2003-2006

Our strategies, which we call "restorative practices," are the basis for a new graduate school, the International Institute for Restorative Practices, that I founded in 2000. https://www.iirp.edu/

We teach educators, youth-serving professionals and others how to be more effective. In 2019, IIRP had trained 25,000 professionals, mostly in the U.S. but also through licensees in Canada, Latin America, Europe and Asia. Our little alternative school has had a national and global impact, beyond our wildest dreams in 1977.

97 - Adlai Stevenson, 1954, http://infoshare1.princeton.edu/libraries/firestone/rbsc/mudd/online_ex/stevenson/adlai1954.html

21. Things You Cannot See

98 - ...unless we turned and became as little children, we would in no way enter the kingdom of Heaven, http://biblehub.com/matthew/18-3.htm

BEYOND THE SCHOOLHOUSE: Learning In A New Reality

99 - Maria Montessori, https://en.wikipedia.org/wiki/Maria_Montessori

100 - Grace and Virginia Kennedy, 6-year-old identical twins who were regarded as severely retarded for most of their lives, https://en.wikipedia.org/wiki/Poto_and_Cabengo

101 - Alex F. Osborn, https://en.wikipedia.org/wiki/Alex_Faickney_Osborn

102 - brainstorming principle, https://en.wikipedia.org/wiki/Brainstorming

22. Reality

103 - George Armstrong Custer, https://en.wikipedia.org/wiki/George_Armstrong_Custer

104 - Thomas B. Marquis, https://en.wikipedia.org/wiki/Thomas_Bailey_Marquis

105 - "Keep the Last Bullet for Yourself," https://www.amazon.com/Keep-last-bullet-yourself-Custers/dp/0917256026

106 - "Reality Therapy: A New Approach to Psychiatry," https://en.wikipedia.org/wiki/Reality_therapy

107 - William Glasser, https://en.wikipedia.org/wiki/William_Glasser

108 - Emile, https://en.wikipedia.org/wiki/Emile,_or_On_Education

109 - Hadfield, https://en.wikipedia.org/wiki/J._A._Hadfield

23. The Revolution

110 - George Gallup III, https://en.wikipedia.org/wiki/George_Gallup

111 - William Irwin Thompson, https://en.wikipedia.org/wiki/William_Irwin_Thompson

112 - "At the Edge of History," https://www.goodreads.com/book/show/5868339-at-the-edge-of-history

113 - Buckminster Fuller, https://en.wikipedia.org/wiki/Buckminster_Fuller

114 - "No More Secondhand God," https://www.amazon.com/No-More-Secondhand-God-Writings/dp/0809302470

Notes

115 - Francis Fitzgerald, https://en.wikipedia.org/wiki/Frances_FitzGerald_(journalist)

116 - "Fire In The Lake," https://en.wikipedia.org/wiki/Fire_in_the_Lake

117 - "I Ching," https://en.wikipedia.org/wiki/I_Ching

24. Learning Systems

118 - "The Learning System," http://www.iirp.edu/images/pdf/92906_THE_LEARNING_SYSTEM7.pdf

119 - Montessori school, https://en.wikipedia.org/wiki/Montessori_education

120 - Despite the remarkable impact of Sesame Street and The Electric Company, federal funding for non-school learning resources may soon be reduced or eliminated completely.

25. Being Our Own Heroes

121 - William Penn, https://en.wikipedia.org/wiki/William_Penn

122 - E.F. Schumacher, https://en.wikipedia.org/wiki/E._F._Schumacher

123 - "Small Is Beautiful: Economics As If People Mattered," https://en.wikipedia.org/wiki/Small_Is_Beautiful

124 - Joseph Catania, http://articles.mcall.com/2003-12-30/news/3499108_1_county-commissioner-minority-commissioner-democratic-party

125 - The Internet and other digital resources provide a remarkable array of learning resources. You can learn language through Babbel (https://my.babbel.com/), watch college lectures and learn a wide array of practical skills. The contractor who renovated a bathroom in our house faced a number of new challenges that he resolved by choosing from the thousands of YouTube videos produced by other contractors, who share their knowledge on a wide range of topics through their homemade videos.

27. Dreaming of a New Reality

126 - Alexei Panshin, https://en.wikipedia.org/wiki/Alexei_Panshin

127 - Cory Panshin, https://en.wikipedia.org/wiki/Cory_Panshin

BEYOND THE SCHOOLHOUSE: Learning In A New Reality

128 - "Star Wars," https://en.wikipedia.org/wiki/Star_Wars

129 - "SF in Dimension: A Book of Explorations," https://www.amazon.com/Dimension-Book-Explorations-Alexei-Panshin/dp/B00225DK1C

130 - The Panshins were quite prescient in their argument, as there is now an established genre in book publishing called "speculative fiction."

131 - George Lucas, https://en.wikipedia.org/wiki/George_Lucas

132 - Jules Verne, https://en.wikipedia.org/wiki/Jules_Verne

133 - Henry David Thoreau, https://en.wikipedia.org/wiki/Henry_David_Thoreau

134 - Alfred Korzybski, https://en.wikipedia.org/wiki/Alfred_Korzybski

135 - Friedrich August Kekule, https://en.wikipedia.org/wiki/August_Kekul%C3%A9

28. A Practical Matter

136 - Community Service Foundation, csfbuxmont.org

29. Future Without Limits

137 - Bertrand Russell, https://en.wikipedia.org/wiki/Bertrand_Russell

Epilogue

138 - article, https://www.washingtonpost.com/news/answer-sheet/wp/2018/01/04/an-open-letter-to-the-people-of-philadelphia-about-their-schools/?utm_term=.d01494110f81

139 - Marshall McLuhan, https://en.wikipedia.org/wiki/Marshall_McLuhan

140 - John C. Pittenger, https://en.wikipedia.org/wiki/John_Pittenger

141 - …alternative schools, group homes and counseling programs for delinquent and at-risk youth in Pennsylvania, csfbuxmont.org

142 - graduate school , iirp.edu

143 - …opted out of standardized testing, opted out of standardized

testing, https://www.usnews.com/opinion/articles/2016-05-09/who-does-the-movement-to-opt-out-of-standardized-testing-help

144 - home-schooled them instead, www.nheri.org/research/research-facts-on-homeschooling.html

145 - "Deschooling Society," https://www.nheri.org/research-facts-on-homeschooling

146 - Learning System article, http://www.iirp.edu/images/pdf/92906_THE_LEARNING_SYSTEM7.pdf

147 - North Star Self-Directed Learning For Teens, https://www.recorder.com/Archives/2015/10/NorthStar-GR-101715

148 - Liberated Learners, liberatedlearners.net

149 - North Star slogan, http://www.northstarteens.org/#learningisnatural

About the Author

Ted Wachtel is a visionary, an educator and a serial entrepreneur, in that order. He has always seen the world as it could be, in its best potential sense.

A man of action, he worked toward that vision first as an educator in the Pennsylvania public school system. Quickly realizing the limitations of what he came to view as an outmoded system that didn't adequately serve all would-be learners, he began working toward a better way; one that addressed the needs of learners who hadn't been able to thrive in the rigid, traditional classroom structure.

From there, he and Susan, his wife, launched a series of projects; some short-lived, but most ongoing. They have organized local political campaigns, founded schools, group homes, counseling and treatment programs for adolescents, an accredited master's degree-granting graduate school, an art museum, a solar housing development, an organic mini-farm, a food cooperative, a book publishing company and more, mostly in the United States but also several projects overseas.

In service of many of these goals, Ted wrote or co-wrote many books, and continues to do so today. Despite having officially retired in 2015, he shows no signs of slowing down his energetic pace, though he does now take more time to spend with loved ones and enjoying the fruits of his many and varied labors over the years.

Building a New Reality is a non-partisan, evidence-based social movement dedicated to the decentralization of power and to participatory decision-making in every facet of society: learning, governance, care, justice, enterprise and spirit.

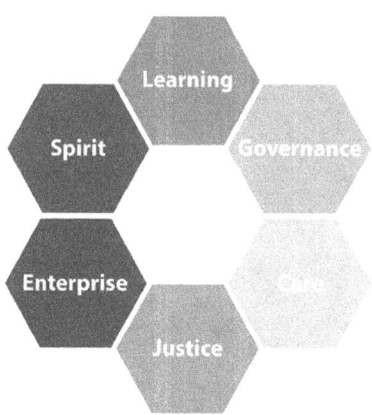

We advocate for more voice and more choice, in exchange for taking more responsibility.

Beyond the Schoolhouse is a manifesto for learning in a new reality.

Visit our website and look around. You can subscribe at the bottom of any page to get blogposts and updates.

Join us.

www.ingramcontent.com/pod-product-compliance
Lightning Source LLC
Chambersburg PA
CBHW072012110526
44592CB00012B/1271